Portraits of Justice

Portraits of Justice

The Wisconsin Supreme Court's First 150 Years

Second Edition

Edited by Trina E. Gray, Karen Leone de Nie, Jennifer Miller, and Amanda K. Todd

Wisconsin Historical Society Press
Madison, Wisconsin

Published by the
Wisconsin Historical Society Press

© 2003 Wisconsin Supreme Court

Publications of the Wisconsin Historical Society Press are available at quantity
discounts for promotions, fund raising, and educational use. Write to the Wisconsin
Historical Society Press, 816 State Street, Madison, WI 53706-1482 for more informa-
tion.

Printed in the United States of America

Image on front cover and page v by Richard G. B. Hanson II
Cover and text design by Roberta H. Couillard

07 06 05 04 03   5 4 3 2 1

Library of Congress Cataloging-in-Publication Data
Portraits of justice : the Wisconsin Supreme Court's first 150
    years / edited by Trina E. Gray   ... [et al.]. -- 2nd ed.
        p. cm.
    Includes bibliographical references and index.
    ISBN 0-87020-345-2
    1. Wisconsin. Supreme Court--History.   2. Judges--Wisconsin
--Biography.   3. Judges--Wisconsin--Portraits.   I. Gray, Trina
E.
KFW2912.P67 2003
347.775'035'09--dc21
                                                    2002155497

Contents

Acknowledgments

Advisors

Senior Judge Thomas E. Fairchild, Judge Paul C. Gartzke, Atty. Eugene O. Gehl, Atty. Joseph A. Melli

Contributors

Kristin M. Crooks, Nathan Roets, Sherie Sasso, Susan A. Thelan, Rebecca L. Wasieleski

A Project of the Wisconsin Legal History Committee

Chief Justice Shirley S. Abrahamson, Wisconsin Supreme Court (co-chair); Atty. Patricia Ballman, president, State Bar of Wisconsin (co-chair); Justice Ann Walsh Bradley, Wisconsin Supreme Court; George Brown, executive director, State Bar of Wisconsin; J. Kent Calder, editorial director, Wisconsin Historical Society Press; Atty. Catherine Cleary, Milwaukee; Atty. Charles Curtis, Madison; Michael Goodman, Wisconsin Academy of Arts, Letters & Sciences; Jack Holzheuter, Wisconsin historian; Professor Gordon Hylton, Marquette Law School; Bobbie Malone, director, Office of School Services, Wisconsin Historical Society; Atty. Gerald Mowris, past president, State Bar of Wisconsin; Atty. Joseph Ranney, Madison; Atty. Edward Reisner, University of Wisconsin Law School; Atty. Joan Bright Rundle, Madison; Atty. Michael Remington, Washington, D.C.; Atty. John Skilton, Madison.

Introduction

The year 2003 marks an important milestone in Wisconsin's legal history. The Wisconsin Supreme Court will celebrate its sesquicentennial, while the State Bar of Wisconsin marks 125 years, and the Wisconsin Court of Appeals celebrates a youthful 25 years.

Creating the Separate Supreme Court

Those who recall the state's sesquicentennial celebration in 1998 might wonder why the Wisconsin Supreme Court's anniversary is five years later. Here is the story: When Wisconsin became the nation's thirtieth state in 1848, the constitutional convention decided to preserve the appellate system that had existed in the territory since 1836. This system brought together the state's circuit court judges—by 1848 there were five—once a year in Madison as a "Supreme Court." They heard appeals of their own decisions, and this practice sometimes created tension. The chief justice of the first court, Alexander Stow, called his fellow justices "consummate blockheads" when they reversed a decision he had made as trial judge.

The new state was to maintain this system for five years and then would have the option to create a separate Supreme Court. In 1852 the state legislature voted to create a separate Supreme Court that would have three members, one of whom would be chief justice. In 1853 the people of Wisconsin chose three men—a New Yorker, a Massachusetts native, and an Irish immigrant—to set a course for the fledgling state's third branch of government. The men were the first justices of the newly formed Wisconsin Supreme Court, and, while they clashed almost immediately on the issue of states' rights and the Fugitive Slave Act, each was known as a man of honor and principle. As the years went by, the Supreme Court increased in size. An 1877 constitutional amendment changed the number of justices from three to five and increased the term of service from six to ten years. In 1903 a constitutional amendment established a court of seven members who serve for ten-year terms, and that structure remains today.

The Men and Women of the Court

In these pages are the stories of the seventy-seven justices who have served on the court since Wisconsin became a state. The Wisconsin Supreme Court originally published *Portraits of Justice* in 1998. This new edition presents biographies on Justices David Prosser, Jr., and Diane S. Sykes, who joined the court in 1998 and 1999, and adds photographs of all seven current justices.

This project began as an effort to learn more about the men whose portraits adorn the walls of the Supreme Court corridors and reception area in the state capitol. The practice of hanging portraits apparently started with the justices who began serving in 1853, the year the separate Supreme Court was created. Upon a justice's death, a ceremony was held and an oil portrait was hung. Since the 1940s most justices have been portrayed in photographs rather than paintings. The portraits of the deceased justices hang in chronological order in the corridors and reception area of the court. The portraits of deceased chief justices, dating from 1853, hang in the marble foyer of the court's Hearing Room.

Publishing the original version of this book in 1998 took some detective work. Other than an oil painting of Mortimer Jackson (1848–1853), which hangs in our private corridor, the court had no portraits of the justices who served in the five years between statehood and the creation of the separate Wisconsin Supreme Court. We were fortunate to track down photographs of four of these early justices at the Wisconsin Historical Society, and they now hang in their rightful places. The fifth of these justices, Wiram Knowlton (1850–1853), remains the only faceless member of the Supreme Court. We know he lived in Prairie du Chien and raised troops for the Mexican War, but no likeness of him has been found. Also missing from the collection was a likeness of Theodore Lewis. He served only twenty days in 1934 before dying of pneumonia. A photograph of Lewis in his World War I uniform was obtained from his niece who lives in the state of Oregon. It now hangs in its proper place.

A Bit of Trivia

The biographies of the justices reveal some interesting and curious facts. Charles Larrabee (1848–1853) was only twenty-eight years old when elected to the circuit court, thereby serving on the Supreme Court. He is the youngest person ever to serve on the Wisconsin Supreme Court. Burr Jones (1920–1926), appointed at age seventy-four, was the oldest justice to begin service on the Supreme Court. Orsamus Cole (1855–1892) served the longest time as a justice of the court, thirty-seven years. Theodore Lewis (1934) served the shortest time—only twenty days—and did not participate in any decisions of the court.

Upon his retirement Edward Fairchild (1929–1957) swore in his son Thomas Fairchild (1957–1966) as a justice of the Supreme Court. Another set of relatives served as justices: Joseph Martin (1934–1946) and John Martin (1948–1962) were uncle and nephew. Four members of the court served together in World War I and were friends: Edward Gehl (1950–1956), Roland Steinle (1954–1958), Joseph Martin (1934–1946), and Theodore Lewis (1934).

Of the seventy-one justices who have served since a separate Supreme Court was established in 1853, thirty-six were not judges prior to their appointment or election to the Supreme Court.

Until 1903, all the justices were born outside Wisconsin. Robert Siebecker (1903–1922) was the first justice born in Wisconsin. The justices have come from diverse parts of the state: twenty-one hailed from Milwaukee County and sixteen from Dane County, but overall the justices have come from twenty-seven of Wisconsin's seventy-two counties.

How Wisconsin Selects Justices

Although political parties nominated the early justices, the framers of the 1848 constitution distanced judicial elections from the general partisan elections. According to the 1848 constitution (a similar provision exists in the present constitution), judicial elections cannot be held at any general elections for state or county officers or within thirty days either before or after such election. The first election for the Supreme Court was held in September 1852. In 1858 the legislature enacted a law calling for judicial elections to be held the first Tuesday in April.

Laws governing judicial elections have continued to change. A 1913 law stated that candidates for judicial office could not be nominated or elected on a party ticket or party designation or principle. Although this provision for nonpartisan elections had not been a part of the statutes before 1913, nonpartisan judicial elections apparently date back to the 1870s in Wisconsin. According to Chief Justice John B. Winslow in *The Story of a Great Court* (1912), the 1878 election marked the first time that justices were elected on a nonpartisan basis.

In March 1949 the legislature provided for primary elections for the office of Supreme Court justice whenever nomination papers for more than two candidates were filed. If no candidate received more than fifty percent of the votes cast in the election, a run-off election between the two candidates who received the highest and second highest number of votes would be held the first Tuesday in May. The person receiving the highest number of votes cast at the May election was deemed elected. The legislature revised the election system in July 1949 to provide that when three or more candidates for justice are nominated, a primary election is held four weeks before the first Tuesday in April. The two candidates who receive the most votes in the primary election are the candidates at the April election. This system is in effect today.

Beginning with the first election for the separate Supreme Court in 1852, the chief justice was elected by the people on a separate ballot. An 1889 state constitutional amendment provided that the justice having the longest continuous service on the court shall be the chief justice. This remains the method of selecting the chief justice.

In 1848 the Wisconsin constitution stated that no person shall be eligible for the office of judge unless at the time of election he is a citizen of the United States, has attained the age of twenty-five years, and is a qualified elector. Only men were qualified electors until the 19th Amendment to the U.S. Constitution was adopted in

1920. Under a 1955 state constitutional amendment, no person may take or hold office as a Supreme Court justice unless he is a qualified elector, licensed to practice law in Wisconsin for at least five years immediately prior to appointment or election. This provision has not changed. The 1955 state constitutional amendment also required that a justice retire at the end of the month in which he attains the age of seventy. In 1968 the constitution was amended to provide that no justice might serve beyond July 31 following the date on which he turned seventy. In 1977 the constitution was amended to provide that the legislature might prescribe by law a retirement age of not less than seventy years. The legislature has not, to date, enacted a mandatory retirement age for justices.

Beginning with the 1848 constitution and continuing today, the governor appoints a justice to the court when a vacancy occurs. The 1848 constitution provided that the appointee continues in the office until a successor is elected and qualified; when elected, the successor serves the unexpired term. In 1953 the constitution was amended to allow the successor to hold office for a ten-year term. A 1903 state constitutional amendment provided that only one justice can run for election in any given year.

Looking Ahead

As Wisconsin Supreme Court Justice Ann Walsh Bradley and Madison attorney Joseph Ranney, an author and legal historian, noted in their *Wisconsin Magazine of History* article "New Cases and Changing Faces: The Wisconsin Supreme Court in 2003" (volume 86, number 2)—from which I have borrowed extensively in writing this introduction—the face and the workings of the Supreme Court have been modified to reflect the changing times, a changed caseload, and the court's enhanced administrative responsibilities.

At the time of the court's centennial, forty-seven men had served as justices. They varied greatly in age and length of service to the court; they were born in different parts of the country and indeed the world and had varying levels of formal education. But they had this in common: they were all men. As the court celebrates its 150th anniversary, three of Wisconsin's seven justices, including the chief justice, are women.

Another significant change in the court is the result of the court reform of 1977, which created the Court of Appeals. The Court of Appeals hears direct appeals from the judgments of the state's circuit courts, thereby freeing the Supreme Court of that role and enabling it to select for review the cases that are most important to the state or to the development of the law.

The cases that the Supreme Court hears and the administrative issues it faces reflect the state of our society. Today's social issues are tomorrow's judicial issues. The state of the economy, regardless of whether it is good or bad, will have an impact on legal and administrative issues, as will technological developments. As the legislature comes to terms with changing social conditions, the court will be responsible for determining the validity or application of such legislation according to state and federal constitutional provisions. Just as the invention of the automobile affected the types of cases seen in the courts, so too will today's cutting-edge technology bring complex legal and ethical issues, especially in the realms of privacy and genetics.

The Supreme Court must also come to terms with difficult administrative issues involving access to courts and the practice of law. As the population of the state continues to grow and diversify, the Supreme Court must find ways to preserve access to the court system. When litigants do not understand what is said or done in court proceedings because of language differences, access is limited. Likewise, access to the courts is limited for those who can hardly afford to put dinner on the table. Bridging language gaps and serving the increasing number of people who represent themselves are high priorities for the court in the years to come.

The past 150 years have brought enormous changes in our society and in the work of the courts. But one element has remained constant: an independent judiciary. Independent judges safeguard our freedoms by deciding cases on the basis of the facts and law, independent of pressure from outside influences. An independent judicial system that dispenses justice fairly, impartially, and according to the rule of law is the cornerstone of our democracy, but it cannot exist without the trust and confidence of the people. The people must trust the courts to help them settle their disputes in a timely, cost-effective, understandable, and fair manner in safe and accessible surroundings in order for the courts to remain strong and viable.

To trust the courts, people must understand the courts. We encourage members of the public—lawyers and non-lawyers alike—to serve on court-related boards and committees and to become involved in volunteer work in the courts. When members of the community work side by side with judges and court staff, we increase the range and scope of services the courts are able to offer. There are about two hundred programs around the state that provide members of the public an opportunity to work in the court system. To learn more about becoming involved in the work of the courts, either through committee work or as a program volunteer, visit the "Connecting to the Courts" section of the court system Web site at www.wicourts.gov. We look forward to hearing from you and to continuing our work to earn and safeguard your trust for the next 150 years and beyond.

Shirley S. Abrahamson, chief justice
Wisconsin Supreme Court
Madison, Wisconsin

Alexander W. Stow

(1805–1854)

Wisconsin Supreme Court Chief Justice

(1848–1851)

"He loved truth for truth's sake, with intense love. He loved justice for itself, with natural and professional devotion."
—Judge Morgan L. Martin, Stow's memorial service (1854)

Wisconsin Historical Society

Alexander Wolcott Stow was born February 5, 1805, in Lowville, New York. He inherited the love of the law from his father, Silas, who was a county court judge and congressman.

At sixteen, Stow attended West Point Military Academy for a year before joining a law firm in his hometown. Later, after traveling extensively in Europe, he practiced law in Rochester, New York. In 1845, he settled on a farm near Fond du Lac in the Wisconsin Territory.

Stow was elected judge for the 4th Judicial Circuit when Wisconsin was admitted to the Union in 1848. Pursuant to the state constitution, he joined the four other circuit judges to form the first Wisconsin Supreme Court. Stow holds a prominent place in Wisconsin's history as the first chief justice of this early court.

Because he was opposed to an elective judiciary, Stow accepted a position on the bench with the pledge that he would not run for a second elected term. Keeping his word, he left the bench after two and a half years of service.

His friend and colleague Judge Morgan L. Martin stated that Stow's refusal to run for election cost the state a great judge and left Stow "comparatively unknown and unappreciated . . . [a] longer judicial career would undoubtedly have placed him in the front rank of American judges."

After completing his term on the Supreme Court, Stow retired. Some written accounts say that he never practiced law again; others say that he pursued a law practice for a few years in Milwaukee and Fond du Lac.

Stow was known as an eccentric man. It was often told that he preferred his meat well ripened before he cooked it. He would hang chickens outside his bedroom window until the legs and bills turned green and the odor of decay pervaded his house.

Stow never married; he died September 14, 1854.

Levi Hubbell
(1808–1876)
Wisconsin Supreme Court Justice
(1848–1853)
Chief Justice
(1851)

Levi Hubbell was the only Wisconsin judge to face an impeachment trial.

Wisconsin Historical Society

Levi Hubbell was born April 15, 1808, in upstate New York. He graduated from Union College and was admitted to the New York Bar in 1827. Hubbell was the adjutant general of New York and a member of the state assembly. He also was editor of a New York newspaper, the *Ontario Messenger.*

In the early 1840s, Hubbell moved to Milwaukee, Wisconsin, and joined a private law firm. In the first judicial election after Wisconsin became a state in 1848, Hubbell was elected circuit judge for the 2nd Judicial Circuit. Pursuant to the state constitution, he joined the four other circuit judges to form the first Wisconsin Supreme Court. In 1851, he became the chief justice of this early court. When a separate Supreme Court was organized in 1853, Hubbell lost the Democratic nomination to the new court and resumed his position as a circuit judge.

In 1853, his opponents, led by Edward G. Ryan, an influential Milwaukee attorney who later became the chief justice of the Wisconsin Supreme Court, sought to impeach Hubbell for judicial misconduct. In a long, highly publicized trial, Ryan accused Hubbell of accepting bribes and hearing cases in circuit court in which he had financial interests. Although Hubbell was acquitted, his reputation was tarnished. He resigned as a circuit judge, stating that the salary of $1,500 a year was too low.

Hubbell was elected to the state assembly in 1863 and served one year. In 1871, he was appointed the U.S. Attorney for the Eastern District of Wisconsin; he served until 1875. He resigned under accusations of misconduct in a government patronage scandal that received national attention. He resumed his law practice in Milwaukee.

Hubbell died December 8, 1876.

Edward V. Whiton
(1805–1859)
Wisconsin Supreme Court Justice
(1848–1859)
Chief Justice
(1853–1859)

"If the judicial ermine and gown in Wisconsin shall drop from other shoulders hereafter as pure and unsullied as from his, we shall have no cause to feel ashamed."
—Justice Samuel Crawford, Whiton's memorial service (1859)

Edward Vernon Whiton was born June 2, 1805, and raised in South Lee, Massachusetts. He attended school and studied law for seven years with a private firm. In 1836, Whiton came to the Wisconsin Territory, where he purchased land and built a cabin near Janesville.

Whiton successfully sought a seat in the first territorial assembly in 1837. He was elected speaker of the assembly in 1839 and published the first collection of territorial laws. The arduous task of recording all of the laws passed by the legislature was a great contribution since no complete record yet existed. Whiton served in the assembly until elected a delegate to the 1848 state Constitutional Convention.

After Wisconsin became a state in 1848, Whiton was elected circuit judge for the 1st Judicial Circuit. Pursuant to the state constitution, he joined the four other circuit judges to form the first Wisconsin Supreme Court.

In 1852, elections were held for a chief justice and two associate justices to comprise a separate Supreme Court beginning in 1853. Wisconsin was a heavily Democratic state at the time. Whiton, representing the Whig party, ran for chief justice against the Democratic candidate, Charles Larrabee, who was also a member of the original Supreme Court. In a very narrow election, Whiton defeated Larrabee and became the first elected chief justice of the separate Supreme Court.

While on the Supreme Court, Whiton played an important role in *Ableman v. Booth* (1854), a highly controversial case involving Milwaukee abolitionist Sherman M. Booth and the Fugitive Slave Act. Whiton and Justice Abram D. Smith defied the federal law and ordered Booth's release from jail. The case was appealed to the U.S. Supreme Court, which overturned the Wisconsin Supreme Court's decision several years later.

Whiton did not live to see the end of the controversy. He left the bench April 12, 1859, and died the same day at the age of fifty-four. Whiton was known as a kind and courteous man, particularly to the younger lawyers who appeared before him. His fellow justices praised his collegiality, integrity, and honesty.

Charles H. Larrabee
(1820–1883)
Wisconsin Supreme Court Justice
(1848–1853)

"As a judge, he was prompt and impartial, and his written opinions bear favorable testimony to his learning and ability; he possesses more than ordinary natural ability; is an impressive public speaker; his manners are free, affable and popular, and is zealous as a partisan and warm and devoted in his friendships."
—Silas U. Pinney, *Sketches of the Judges of the First Supreme Court* (1876)

Wisconsin Historical Society

Charles Hathaway Larrabee was born in Rome, New York, on November 9, 1820. His family moved to Cincinnati, Ohio, where he attended Granville College from 1834 to 1836.

Before studying law, Larrabee worked as an engineer and helped survey for the Little Miami railroad. He was admitted to the bar in 1841. Three years later, Larrabee moved to Chicago, where he served one term as city attorney and edited the *Democratic Advocate.*

In 1847, Larrabee moved to Horicon, Wisconsin. Later that year, Dodge County elected him to be a delegate to the 1848 state Constitutional Convention.

Larrabee was elected circuit judge for the 3rd Judicial Circuit in 1848. Pursuant to the state constitution, he joined the other four circuit judges to form the first Wisconsin Supreme Court. He was only twenty-eight years old at the time, making him the youngest justice ever to serve on the state's Supreme Court.

When a separate Supreme Court was organized in 1853, Larrabee ran as a Democrat for the office of chief justice but was defeated by the older and more experienced Whig candidate, Edward V. Whiton. Larrabee continued as a circuit judge until 1858, when he was elected to the U.S. House of Representatives.

At the outbreak of the Civil War in 1861, Larrabee was among the first to volunteer and was appointed major of the 5th Wisconsin Infantry. A year later, he was promoted to colonel of the 24th Regiment.

Larrabee resigned from the military in 1863 and moved west. He practiced law and was involved in public affairs in the Oregon, California, and Washington Territories and helped draft the state constitution in Washington.

Larrabee was married to Minerva Norton. He died in Los Angeles on January 20, 1883.

Mortimer M. Jackson
(1809–1889)
Wisconsin Supreme Court Justice
(1848–1853)

"In all his social, personal and official relations, Judge Jackson was eminently a polite, courtly, dignified gentleman of the old school; treating at all times his associates and acquaintances with the kindest and most respectful consideration."
—Silas U. Pinney, Jackson's memorial service (1891)

Mortimer Melville Jackson was born March 5, 1809, in Rensselaerville, New York. He attended college in New York City.

While a merchant in New York, Jackson became an active member and vice president of the Mercantile Library Association. In 1834, he organized a delegation to the Young Men's New York State Whig Convention.

Jackson moved to Mineral Point, Wisconsin, in 1838. He established a law practice and settled disputes in the lead mining industry. In 1841, he was appointed attorney general of the Wisconsin Territory and held the office until 1846.

In 1848, Jackson was elected circuit judge for the 5th Judicial Circuit, covering one-third of the state. Pursuant to the state constitution, he joined the four other circuit judges to form the first Wisconsin Supreme Court. Jackson traveled vast distances to fill his duties as circuit judge and Supreme Court justice.

When Levi Hubbell's term as chief justice expired in 1851, Jackson was voted chief justice by his colleagues. He declined to serve in favor of Edward V. Whiton. Jackson continued his dual role as a circuit judge and Supreme Court justice until the state organized a separate Supreme Court in 1853.

Early in the Civil War, President Abraham Lincoln appointed Jackson as U.S. diplomat to Canada, where he served for twenty-one years. Jackson returned to Madison in 1884. In his will, he donated $20,000 to the University of Wisconsin Law School to create a professorship in his name.

Jackson was married to Catherine Garr. He died October 13, 1889.

Wiram Knowlton
(1816–1863)
Wisconsin Supreme Court Justice
(1850–1853)

"He was a man of good natural talents, and discharged the duties of his office with commendable ability; and his judicial integrity was unquestioned."
—Silas U. Pinney, *Sketches of the Judges of the First Supreme Court* (1876)

Wiram Knowlton was born January 24, 1816, in Canandaigua, New York. In 1837, he moved to Janesville, Wisconsin, and began to study law. He was admitted to the bar in 1840 and opened a law practice in Prairie du Chien, where he served on the territorial council from 1844 to 1846.

At the outbreak of the Mexican War, Knowlton raised a company of volunteers and served as captain. His troops were never ordered to Mexico but were assigned to Fort Crawford for detached frontier duty.

In 1850, Knowlton was elected circuit judge for the newly created 6th Judicial Circuit, which extended from the Wisconsin River to Lake Superior. As a circuit judge, he also served as a justice on the Wisconsin Supreme Court until a separate Supreme Court was organized in 1853. Knowlton was known not as a great judge, but as a good man.

Knowlton remained in the judiciary as a circuit judge until 1856, when he resumed his law practice in Prairie du Chien.

Knowlton never married and did not have children. He died June 27, 1863, at the age of forty-seven.

After much searching, the Supreme Court has been unable to obtain a photograph or painting of Wiram Knowlton. He remains the only faceless member of the Supreme Court.

Timothy O. Howe

(1816–1883)

Wisconsin Supreme Court Justice

(1851–1853)

"Judge Howe is an able debater, has a ready command of language, with all the resources of extemporaneous oratory, and appears best in the sudden exigencies of debate."
—Silas U. Pinney, *Sketches of the Judges of the First Supreme Court* (1876)

Wisconsin Historical Society

Timothy Otis Howe was born February 24, 1816, in Livermore, Maine. He attended Readfield Seminary in Readfield, Maine, and studied law with local judges. In 1839, Howe was admitted to the Vermont Bar and began practicing law in Readfield.

In 1845, he was elected to the Vermont legislature. Shortly thereafter, Howe moved to Green Bay, Wisconsin, and opened a law office. He was an ardent Whig and admirer of Henry Clay and became interested in political issues. He launched an unsuccessful campaign for U.S. Congress in 1848.

Howe was elected circuit judge for the 4th Judicial Circuit in 1850 and began serving in 1851. As a circuit judge, he also served as a justice on the Wisconsin Supreme Court until a separate Supreme Court was organized in 1853. He left the Supreme Court but remained a circuit judge until 1855, when he resumed his law practice.

Howe ran unsuccessfully for the U.S. Senate in 1857. His defeat was attributed in part to his refusal to support states' rights, a popular position in the free North that states can disregard a federal law if they do not agree with it. The southern states later used the same doctrine when they seceded from the Union.

In 1861, Howe won election to the U.S. Senate. He supported emancipation, black suffrage, and impeaching President Andrew Johnson.

During Howe's Senate term, President Ulysses S. Grant offered him the position of chief justice of the U.S. Supreme Court. However, Howe declined the offer because he feared his successor to the Senate would be a Democrat. It was more important to him that the Republicans retained a seat in the Senate than for him to join the U.S. Supreme Court.

Howe lost his senatorial seat in 1877, but he continued to serve the nation as commissioner to the Paris International Monetary Conference until 1881. That year he was appointed U.S. postmaster general, a position he held until his death on March 25, 1883.

Samuel Crawford
(1820–1860)
Wisconsin Supreme Court Justice
(1853–1855)

"Judge Crawford was a most genial and accomplished gentleman, chivalrous in his disposition, and of the strictest honor and integrity. He had a heart full of warm sympathies and generous impulses, and as a man and citizen was greatly beloved."
—Calvert Spensley, Crawford's portrait hanging (1904)

Samuel Crawford was born April 20, 1820, in Ballibay, Ireland. He was educated by his father and came to the United States in 1840. In 1841, he moved from New York to Galena, Illinois, where his brothers lived. He studied law at a private firm and was admitted to the Illinois Bar in 1844. He established a successful law practice in Galena but soon moved to Mineral Point, Wisconsin, to form a law partnership with David W. Jones (who later became Wisconsin secretary of state).

When a separate Wisconsin Supreme Court was created in 1853, Crawford was elected to serve as one of the three justices. The law creating the Supreme Court included a provision for selecting a chief justice and assigned a long term for one associate justice and a short term for the other. Crawford was given the shorter term, which expired June 1855.

His opinion in *Ableman v. Booth* (1854) is believed to have cost him reelection in 1855. The case questioned the constitutionality of the federal Fugitive Slave Act, which required runaway slaves to be returned to their masters. Crawford wrote that Wisconsin had to enforce the Fugitive Slave Act. His opinion was unpopular because of the strong antislavery sentiment in Wisconsin.

After losing the election, Crawford pursued private practice in Mineral Point. He was twice defeated in bids for public office—the first for the U.S. Congress in 1856 and the second for Wisconsin attorney general in 1859.

Crawford was married to Jane Sweet and had four children. He died February 28, 1860.

Abram D. Smith

(1811–1865)

Wisconsin Supreme Court Justice

(1853–1859)

*"He had an abiding love for and devotion to the great principles of civil liberty and
natural justice; and I believe it was the strongest desire of his soul that every
human being, however degraded, should enjoy his natural rights."*

—Justice Orsamus Cole, Smith's memorial service (1865)

Little is known about the life of Abram
Daniel Smith. He came to the Wisconsin
Territory from New York in 1842 and
practiced law in Milwaukee. He was elected
one of the three justices for the newly created
1853 Wisconsin Supreme Court and served
until 1859.

Smith wrote a famous but controversial
opinion in *Ableman v. Booth* (1854), which the
U.S. Supreme Court later overturned. He
wrote that the federal Fugitive Slave Act violated states' rights, and he declared it unconstitutional.

In 1856, Smith was implicated in a major
railroad scandal in Wisconsin. Smith admitted
receiving $10,000 from one of Wisconsin's
major railroad promoters. Governor Coles
Bashford and dozens of legislators were also implicated.

Following his term on the Supreme Court, Smith practiced law in Wisconsin
until the outbreak of the Civil War, when he accepted a government appointment in
South Carolina.

Smith was described as patient, kindhearted, and courteous, particularly to
younger members of the bar.

He died June 3, 1865.

Orsamus Cole
(1819–1903)
Wisconsin Supreme Court Justice
(1855–1892)
Chief Justice
(1880–1892)

*"Of Chief Justice Cole it was literally true that in every instance
it was the office that sought the man."*
—Judge George Clementson, Cole's memorial service (1903)

Orsamus Cole was born August 23, 1819, in Cazenovia, New York. He graduated from Union College in 1843 and was admitted to the New York Bar in 1845. Later that year, Cole moved to Potosi, a small mining town in southwestern Wisconsin, where he began a law practice and a career in politics.

Cole was elected by Grant County voters as their delegate to the 1848 state Constitutional Convention. One report of the convention stated: "At the close of the session but few men stood higher in the estimation of their fellows than did Orsamus Cole."

A year later, Cole was elected to the 31st U.S. Congress. He witnessed several famous congressional speeches, including the pro-Union addresses of Whig leader Henry Clay. Cole also became a friend of President Zachary Taylor.

During Cole's term in Congress, constant division existed along party and sectional lines regarding slavery. Clay proposed the Compromise of 1850, which consisted of five points of reconciliation, one of which called for a more stringent law regarding fugitive slaves. Cole opposed proslavery legislation and voted against the Fugitive Slave Act, deserting his party and Clay. Cole soon realized that the life of a congressman was not for him. After his term, he resumed the practice of law in Wisconsin.

Cole was elected to the Wisconsin Supreme Court in 1855. After serving as justice for twenty-five years, he became the chief justice and held that position for twelve years. With thirty-seven years on the bench, he is the longest-serving justice in Wisconsin history. He participated in cases reported in seventy-seven volumes of the *Wisconsin Reports*.

In January 1892, Cole retired from the Supreme Court and moved to Milwaukee. He had married twice; he died May 5, 1903.

Luther S. Dixon
(1825–1891)
Wisconsin Supreme Court Chief Justice
(1859–1874)

"Justice Dixon . . . wrote a splendid opinion [In re: Booth] in support of the decision of the supreme court of the United States, proclaiming the supremacy of the federal laws and courts over those of the several states. This, of course, was not only sound legal reasoning, but it was the work of a fearless, courageous, intellectually honest judge."
—John P. McGalloway, Wisconsin Supreme Court Centennial (1953)

Luther Swift Dixon was born June 17, 1825, in Milton, Vermont. He was educated at a military school in Norwich, Vermont. He then taught school and later studied law with a distinguished lawyer and politician. He was admitted to the Vermont Bar in 1850.

In 1851, Dixon moved to Portage, Wisconsin. He was twice elected district attorney for Columbia County between 1851 and 1855 and was appointed judge for the 9th Judicial Circuit in 1858.

In 1859, Governor Alexander Randall appointed Dixon to fill the seat of the late Chief Justice Edward V. Whiton. At age thirty-three, Dixon was the youngest chief justice to serve on the Wisconsin Supreme Court and remains so today.

While on the Supreme Court, Dixon was involved in the *Ableman v. Booth* (1854) case. In 1859, the U.S. Supreme Court reversed the Wisconsin Supreme Court's ruling that the Fugitive Slave Act was unconstitutional. Dixon and his colleagues Chief Justice Orsamus Cole and Justice Byron Paine grappled with their duty of filing the U.S. Supreme Court's mandate. Paine did not vote since he was a lawyer in the case. Cole voted not to file the mandate, and Dixon, who concluded that the U.S. Supreme Court had the power to reverse the state court, voted to file the mandate. Dixon feared that if a state could overrule the federal government, it could render the federal government ineffective. However, no action could be taken with the Wisconsin Supreme Court divided. To this day, the mandate has not been filed.

Months after writing the Booth opinion, Dixon faced election to the bench and won by a narrow margin. He was reelected in 1863 and resigned in 1874 to practice law, which was more lucrative than his judicial salary of $2,500 a year. Even in those days, $2,500 was meager and justices had to borrow to meet living expenses. It was widely known that Dixon had financial difficulties and needed to earn more money to pay off personal debts.

During the next five years, Dixon declined a Republican nomination for the U.S. Senate, served as counsel for the Wisconsin railroads, participated in cases concerning railroad regulations, and served as prosecuting counsel for the federal government in the "Whiskey Ring" scandals of 1874 and 1875.

Dixon had health problems that forced him to move to Denver, Colorado, in 1879. He returned to Milwaukee in 1891 and died December 6 of that year.

Byron Paine
(1827–1871)
Wisconsin Supreme Court Justice
(1859–1864; 1867–1871)

"Without the states there can be no union; the abrogation of state sovereignty is not a dissolution of the union, but an absorption of its elements. He is the true man, the faithful officer, who is ready to assert and guard every jot of power rightfully belonging to each, and to resist the slightest encroachment or assumption of power on the part of either."
—Byron Paine, counsel in *Ableman v. Booth* (1854)

B yron Paine was born October 10, 1827, in Painesville, Ohio. In 1847, he and his father moved to Milwaukee, Wisconsin, where Paine studied law. He was admitted to the Wisconsin Bar in 1849.

As a young lawyer, Paine was a close friend of Sherman M. Booth, a Wisconsin abolitionist who was arrested for violating the Fugitive Slave Act after helping to free Joshua Glover, a fugitive slave from Missouri who was arrested in Racine. In 1854, Paine represented Booth, without pay, in the famous *Ableman v. Booth* case. Paine appeared before the Wisconsin Supreme Court and "made one of the clearest, most conclusive and most eloquent arguments against the constitutionality of the fugitive slave law made in any court in the country," said Justice Harlow S. Orton at Paine's memorial service. Paine won the case, becoming the only lawyer to successfully argue in a state court that the Fugitive Slave Act violated the sovereignty of the northern states. The U.S. Supreme Court later reversed the Wisconsin Supreme Court's ruling.

Edward G. Ryan, opposing counsel in the *Booth* case and later chief justice of the Wisconsin Supreme Court, said of Paine's work on the case: "The first opportunity I had of forming an estimate of his high ability, was in the famous case under the fugitive slave act, in 1854 and 1855. He was employed for the defendant; I, for the United States. We both brought to the case, not only ordinary professional zeal, but all the prejudices of all our lives. He was a frank and manly abolitionist. I was as decidedly what was called pro-slavery. We were both thoroughly in earnest . . . I thought him a fanatic. He probably thought me one. Possibly we both were."

In 1856, Paine served as the clerk of the state senate. In 1857, he was elected judge in Milwaukee County and served until his election to the Wisconsin Supreme Court in 1859. In August 1864, near the end of the Civil War, he resigned from the bench to join the military. He was appointed lieutenant colonel of the Wisconsin Volunteer Infantry's 43rd Regiment.

There was much speculation as to why Paine chose to resign from the bench at such a late stage in the war. Chief Justice John B. Winslow wrote that Paine had been elected to the Supreme Court based on his strong states' rights position, a position that became very unpopular at the outbreak of the Civil War. The states' rights movement laid the groundwork for the southern states' secession from the Union. Winslow wrote that enlisting in the military was "the only effective way to prove his [Paine's] absolute loyalty to the Union and his hatred of secession. . . ."

At the end of the war, Paine returned to Milwaukee to practice law. Two years later, he was appointed to the Wisconsin Supreme Court to fill the vacancy created by Justice Jason Downer's resignation.

Paine was an avid reader outside of the law and enjoyed studying theology. He and his wife, Clarissa, had three sons. Paine served on the Supreme Court until his health failed in November 1870; he died January 13, 1871.

Jason Downer

(1813–1883)

Wisconsin Supreme Court Justice

(1864–1867)

"And he gave his whole heart and soul and energy to the study and practice of his chosen profession. They seemed to be his delight by day and his solace by night."
—Chief Justice Orsamus Cole, Downer's memorial service (1884)

Jason Downer was born September 9, 1813, in Sharon, Vermont. In 1838, he graduated from Dartmouth College. He moved to Louisville, Kentucky, where he studied law and was admitted to the bar.

In 1842, Downer moved to Milwaukee. He was one of the original founders of the *Milwaukee Sentinel* and served as the editor for a time, before Rufus King was named editor.

Downer spent most of his life practicing law in Milwaukee. He was appointed to the Wisconsin Supreme Court in 1864 to fill the vacancy created by Justice Byron Paine's resignation to join the U.S. Army. Downer was elected to the court in 1865 but disliked judicial duties. He stepped down from the bench in 1867.

Although Downer served only three years on the Supreme Court, he was well respected by his fellow justices. Chief Justice Orsamus Cole said of Downer's style: "He conscientiously investigated each case for himself and mastered all its facts. . . . He had a strong sense of justice, and thought the rights of parties would be the most fully protected and secured by a rigid adherence to settled principles."

After leaving the Supreme Court, Downer returned to private law practice in Milwaukee and was involved in numerous business ventures. He became a wealthy man and left the bulk of his estate to the Wisconsin Female College at Fox Lake. This college was later combined with Milwaukee College and renamed Milwaukee-Downer College.

Downer died September 1, 1883.

William P. Lyon
(1822–1913)
Wisconsin Supreme Court Justice
(1871–1894)
Chief Justice
(1892–1894)

"Personally he was kindhearted, just, wholesome, companionable, modest. In the judicial office he was splendidly equipped for his task both because of his fine physique and the great breadth of his experience in the world's affairs."
—William M. Kearney, Lyon's memorial service (1913)

William Penn Lyon was born October 28, 1822, in Chatham, New York. He attended public school and worked as an assistant in his father's store. At age fifteen, he taught in the local public school for a salary of fifteen dollars per week. His family moved to Walworth County, Wisconsin, in 1841, and he began studying law. After being admitted to the bar, he became a justice of the peace for what is now the Town of Lyons.

In 1850, Lyon moved to Burlington and formed a law partnership. He moved to Racine County in 1855 and was elected its district attorney. He was later elected to the state legislature and served as speaker in 1855 and 1856.

Many soldiers from Racine were either injured or killed in the Battle of Bull Run in 1861. As a result, the citizens of Racine held a massive meeting and raised money to support volunteer troops. Lyon enlisted and was elected the captain of a company in the Eagle Regiment. He was later promoted to major and then brigadier general.

After his first battle, Lyon wrote to his wife: "You ask me how I felt when going into battle. It is hard to analyze my feelings. I did not forget the danger to myself, but I was cool and self-possessed. The predominant thought was that possibly many of the brave men who followed me would never return, and I wondered—if I came out alive—over which of them the scalding tears would fall ere the sun should set."

While stationed in Huntsville, Tennessee, in March 1865, Lyon received a telegram from Janesville, Wisconsin, announcing that he had been nominated circuit judge for the 1st Judicial Circuit. Lyon was surprised, especially because his opponent was a well-known incumbent judge. He accepted the nomination and won election by a wide margin. He resigned from the army in 1865 and returned to Wisconsin to fill his judgeship.

In 1865, the 1st Judicial Circuit was one of the largest and busiest circuits in the state. Lyon took few vacations or holidays in his six years on the trial bench. He traveled the five counties in his circuit year round. Although he loved the work, after years of outdoor life and vigorous exercise in the army it was a difficult adjustment.

Lyon ran unsuccessfully for U.S. Congress in 1870 but was appointed to the Wisconsin Supreme Court by Governor Lucius Fairchild in January 1871. He was subsequently elected, reelected, and became the chief justice in 1892. His opinions span fifty-nine volumes of the *Wisconsin Reports.*

Upon retiring from the Supreme Court in 1894 against the wishes of many friends and colleagues, he was appointed to the State Board of Control of State Charitable, Penal and Reformatory Institutions.

Lyon was married to Adella Duncombe. Toward the end of his life, he moved to California to be near his two children. He died April 4, 1913.

Edward G. Ryan
(1810–1880)
Wisconsin Supreme Court Chief Justice
(1874–1880)

"There's yet a hope beyond deceiving, and yet a home beyond the tomb;
where rests the soul,
—oh never grieving; It is, it is the spirit's home. . . ."
—Justice Edward G. Ryan's poem "The exile; a duet."

E dward George Ryan was born in County Meath, Ireland, on November 13, 1810. He attended a Jesuit college outside Dublin before coming to the United States at age twenty. He settled in New York City and studied law. In 1836, he moved to Chicago, where he practiced law, edited a newspaper, and was a city attorney.

Ryan moved to Racine, Wisconsin, in 1842. He was elected to the 1846 state Constitutional Convention and played a key role in drafting Wisconsin's first constitution, which the territory's voters rejected. In 1848, he moved his law practice to Milwaukee and was active in the political battles of the day.

As a lawyer, Ryan was involved in many important cases in Wisconsin history. In 1853, he was the special prosecutor in the impeachment proceedings against Milwaukee Circuit Judge and former state Supreme Court Chief Justice Levi Hubbell. In 1854, Ryan prosecuted abolitionist Sherman M. Booth for violating the Fugitive Slave Act. Booth was represented by Byron Paine, who also became a Wisconsin Supreme Court justice. A year later, Ryan represented Coles Bashford in the famous *Bashford v. Barstow* case in which the Wisconsin Supreme Court removed an incumbent governor from office after it was discovered that his victory resulted from fraud.

Ryan had a quick and violent temper that alienated colleagues and clients alike. As a result, by the spring of 1870 he was nearly penniless. Later that year, he was elected city attorney of Milwaukee; he held the post for three years. In June 1874, Ryan was appointed to the Wisconsin Supreme Court. His personality and outspoken convictions made his appointment controversial. His intelligence and legal insight made him suitable for the job.

He wrote what was perhaps his best-known opinion in response to Rhoda Lavinia Goodell's application to be admitted to practice law before the Wisconsin Supreme Court. The Supreme Court denied her motion, and Ryan wrote that the profession of law was "unfit for female character."

Justice Orsamus Cole said that despite Ryan's well-known temper, he treated his colleagues with kindness, respect, and courtesy in the conference room.

Ryan's disposition affected his personal life. His second wife, Caroline, left him in 1872, taking their seven children with her.

On October 13, 1880, Ryan withdrew from a case because he had earlier represented one of the parties. The next day, he sent word to his colleagues that he felt ill. He died October 19, 1880.

David Taylor

(1818–1891)

Wisconsin Supreme Court Justice

(1878–1891)

"His works which live after him, better than words of praise, exemplify the man who so long and so worthily served the state and his fellow-men."
—W. H. Seaman, Taylor's memorial service (1891)

David Taylor was born March 11, 1818, in Carlisle, New York. He graduated from Union College in 1841 and was admitted to the bar in 1844. He practiced law in New York for two years before moving to the Wisconsin Territory.

Taylor started a successful law partnership in Sheboygan in 1846 and served clients from all over the state for eleven years. Taylor was known as a steadfast worker and a contemplative man whose mind was always running. "Relaxation and recreation were nothing to him," Attorney W. H. Seaman said. "Seemingly, he never desired either; holidays and vacations were merely interruptions."

At Taylor's memorial service, Seaman, who had first met Taylor in 1849, told this story: They were young lawyers trying a lawsuit before a judge in Sheboygan County. The trial lasted late into the evening, and they both stayed overnight in town. The next morning, Taylor and Seaman were traveling many miles home. Taylor was on horseback and passed Seaman, who was walking. Taylor stopped, dismounted, and said to Seaman: "You take my horse and ride awhile, I'd like the change." They shared the horse all day and, at the end of the trip, simply said goodbye. Their paths continued to cross for the next forty-two years.

Taylor served in the state assembly in 1853 and in the state senate from 1855 to 1856. As a legislator, he was "quiet, careful and attentive." He was appointed judge for the 4th Judicial Circuit in 1857 and held the position for the next twelve years. In 1869, he returned to the state senate for another term.

After retiring from the circuit bench, Taylor resumed his law practice in Sheboygan and later settled in Fond du Lac. An accomplished lawyer, Taylor was one of the revisers responsible for the Revised Statutes of 1858. In 1871, Taylor produced an excellent compilation of all state public statutory law with valuable annotations which became known as *Taylor's Statutes*. When the state conducted another revision in 1878, Taylor was named president of the revision commission.

In 1878, a state constitutional amendment increased the number of Supreme Court justices from three to five, and Taylor was elected justice. He was reelected to a second term and remained a justice until his death on April 3, 1891. At his memorial service, it was said there was no man in the state whose knowledge of the law could be compared with Taylor's.

Harlow S. Orton
(1817–1895)
Wisconsin Supreme Court Justice
(1878–1895)
Chief Justice
(1894–1895)

"In his intercourse with the people of every class he was gentle, sympathetic, and kindly, and he was gallant and courteous in a strong degree. His radiant smiles and his ringing cheery voice were in themselves mediums of encouragement and hope to all who came within the circle of his presence."
—Judge E. W. Keyes, Orton's memorial service (1895)

Harlow South Orton was born in Niagara County, New York, on November 23, 1817. He was educated at the Hamilton Academy and Madison University in New York.

In 1837, Orton became a schoolteacher in Kentucky. Later that year, he left teaching to join his brother Myron, a lawyer, in Indiana. Orton was admitted to the bar in 1838. He practiced law until 1843, when the governor of Indiana appointed him probate judge for Porter County. Four years later, Orton moved to the Wisconsin Territory and began practicing law in Milwaukee.

Orton moved to Madison in 1852 and served as the private secretary and legal adviser to Governor Leonard J. Farwell. He was elected to the state assembly in 1854. In 1856, he served as defense counsel in *Bashford v. Barstow*, in which the Wisconsin Supreme Court removed an incumbent governor from office because his election had resulted from fraud.

In 1859, Orton was appointed judge for the 9th Judicial Circuit to fill the vacancy left by Luther S. Dixon, who became a Wisconsin Supreme Court justice. Orton resigned as circuit judge in 1865 and returned to private law practice. He was elected to the state assembly in 1869 and reelected in 1871. He ran for U.S. Congress in 1876 but was defeated by a narrow margin. Orton served as dean of the University of Wisconsin Law School from 1869 to 1874 and served one term as mayor of Madison, in 1877.

Also in 1877, Wisconsin amended its constitution to create two more seats on the Supreme Court, and Orton was elected. Orton became the chief justice when Chief Justice William Lyon retired in 1894.

Orton was on the Wisconsin Supreme Court until he died on July 4, 1895. He and his wife, Elizabeth Cheney, had four children.

John B. Cassoday
(1830–1907)
Wisconsin Supreme Court Justice
(1880–1907)
Chief Justice
(1895–1907)

"To him there was a sacredness about judicial decisions. He respected the precedents
found in the adjudicated cases, and depended upon them more than upon philosophical
consideration of the law involved in the case which he had under consideration."
—E. Ray Stevens, proceedings of the State Historical Society of Wisconsin (1908)

John B. Cassoday was born July 7, 1830, in Fairfield, New York. At an early age, he moved with his widowed mother to Pennsylvania. In 1856, he graduated from Albany Law School in New York State; he later moved to Janesville, Wisconsin, to establish a law practice.

During his twenty-three years of private practice, Cassoday was twice elected to the Wisconsin assembly and served one term as speaker. He was a delegate to the National Republican Convention in 1864 (when President Abraham Lincoln was nominated for a second term) and again in 1880. He became chief justice in 1895.

Cassoday was appointed to the Wisconsin Supreme Court in 1880. He took his appointment seriously, E. Ray Stevens said at the proceedings of the Wisconsin Historical Society in 1908: "Upon his appointment to the bench he gave up active participation in affairs outside the courtroom; his church, [the] State Historical Society, and the State University standing almost alone as exceptions to this rule of conduct."

Cassoday's association with the Wisconsin Historical Society included nearly twenty years as a member of its Board of Curators and a term as its vice-president in 1896. He gave generous financial support to its library and museum. His involvement at the University of Wisconsin was equally impressive; he taught constitutional law there for eighteen years.

Cassoday and his wife, Mary Spalding, had five children. He died December 30, 1907.

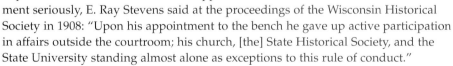

John B. Winslow
(1851–1920)
Wisconsin Supreme Court Justice
(1891–1920)
Chief Justice
(1907–1920)

"The [legal] profession is overrun with money-makers, who regard it only as a business by which money is made, with little or no thought of the quality of the means used. We greatly need many more lawyers who regard the profession as a ministry in the temple of Justice."
—Chief Justice John B. Winslow (1912)

John Bradley Winslow was born October 4, 1851, to parents of colonial ancestry. After living in New York and Ohio, his family moved to Racine, Wisconsin, where his father ran a bookstore for twenty-five years.

In 1871, Winslow received a bachelor's degree from Racine College; he later joined its faculty as an instructor of Greek. Winslow graduated from the University of Wisconsin Law School in 1875. He served as Racine city attorney for three years. In 1883, the thirty-two-year-old Winslow was elected a circuit court judge for Racine, Kenosha, and Walworth Counties. He served in this capacity until he was elected to the Wisconsin Supreme Court in 1891.

Winslow served on the Supreme Court for twenty-nine years, the last thirteen years as chief justice. During his tenure, he participated in approximately ten thousand cases appearing in nearly ninety-two volumes of the *Wisconsin Reports.* He served for many years as president of the American Institute of Criminology.

Winslow also taught at the University of Wisconsin Law School. A faculty member noted: "Winslow believed that as the law touches every human interest, lawyers should be trained in economics, history, the philosophy of law and particularly in a knowledge of other systems of law, such as the Roman law which governs more than half the civilized globe."

In 1912, Winslow completed his book, *The Story of a Great Court.* At first he intended to write a brief history of the Supreme Court. However, he found that the younger members of the bar lacked an understanding of the "remarkable men who sat upon the Supreme Court in the early years of the state. . . ." His paper turned into more than four hundred pages of rich text on the history of the Wisconsin Supreme Court.

Winslow and his wife, Agnes Clancy, had two sons and four daughters. Winslow died July 13, 1920.

Silas U. Pinney
(1833–1899)
Wisconsin Supreme Court Justice
(1892–1898)

"To be at his best, he must be convinced that truth and justice were with him."
—Henry Lewis, Pinney's memorial service (1899)

Silas U. Pinney was born in Rockdale, Pennsylvania, on March 3, 1833. Just after Pinney's thirteenth birthday, his family moved to Wisconsin and settled on a farm in Dane County. Pinney received no formal education in Wisconsin but spent his free time reading and studying. Before turning twenty, Pinney had studied fundamental law books and acted as legal counsel for his neighbors. He moved to Iowa to study in a private law office. He soon returned to Wisconsin and was admitted to the bar in April 1854.

Pinney became known throughout the state as an expert in legal procedure and had an active law practice. Upon his death in 1899, it was believed that he had argued more cases before the Wisconsin Supreme Court than any other lawyer in the state. In the one hundred volumes of the *Wisconsin Reports* printed by the time of his death, his name appeared as either counsel or justice in all but the first two volumes.

In 1872, Pinney gathered the opinions of the territorial Supreme Court and the original state Supreme Court and published them in three volumes called *Pinney's Wisconsin Reports*. The first volume includes Pinney's written history of the Wisconsin Territory.

Before winning election to the Wisconsin Supreme Court in 1891, Pinney served in the state legislature and was mayor of Madison. While mayor, he was instrumental in establishing the second free public library in the state. Pinney's remarkable career as a lawyer led his colleagues throughout the state to nominate him to the bench upon Chief Justice Orsamus Cole's retirement.

He was an entertaining and witty master of the spoken language and was as popular a jurist as he was a lawyer. His opinions were described as "an enduring monument to his ability as a jurist, his strong grasp of legal principles, his clear and cogent reasoning."

Failing health forced Pinney to resign from the Supreme Court in November 1898. During his successful career, he had suffered many personal tragedies. He and his wife, Mary, had one son, Clarence, who died at age twenty; Pinney's daughter Bessie died in a horse-drawn carriage accident. Pinney died April 1, 1899.

Alfred W. Newman
(1834–1898)
Wisconsin Supreme Court Justice
(1894–1898)

"On the bench he struck at once for the heart and justice of the case before him. . . . In a trial his thought steered him through cobwebs and shams and enabled him to go right to the point."
—J. W. Losey, Newman's memorial service (1898)

Alfred W. Newman was born April 5, 1834, in Durham, New York. At thirteen, Newman attended a trial where his father was called as a witness. It was then, Newman later explained, that he decided to become a lawyer. Newman graduated from Hamilton College in 1857. He then studied in a private law firm and was admitted to the New York Bar.

In 1858, Newman moved to Wisconsin and settled in Trempealeau County. He practiced law and became a county judge in 1860. He held that position until 1867, when he was elected district attorney, a post he held for eight years. Newman was elected to the state assembly in 1863 and to the state senate in 1868 and 1869.

Newman was elected judge for the newly created 13th Judicial Circuit in 1876. He moved to the 6th Judicial Circuit in 1878 and served for the next sixteen years. Attorney Burr W. Jones said of Newman's work on the trial court: "There is no doubt that his long service as a circuit judge was to him a labor of love. On the circuit, he thoroughly enjoyed the study of human nature, the sharp contrasts between the tragedy and the comedy of life."

Newman won election to the Wisconsin Supreme Court in 1893 and began his term in 1894. Two years later, Newman suffered a stroke. Although the stroke left him slightly speech impaired and partially paralyzed for a few months, he recovered well and returned to work.

On the morning of January 11, 1898, Newman slipped on a patch of ice while walking to the Supreme Court from his home. He suffered a skull fracture and died the next day. Newman was married and had three children.

Roujet D. Marshall
(1847–1922)
Wisconsin Supreme Court Justice
(1895–1918)

"The ideal of judicial procedure is one enabling courts to prevent and redress wrongs with the greatest possible promptness, certainty, and economy in public and private expense—fully vindicating the crowning idea of human justice, 'There is no wrong without a remedy'."
—Justice Roujet D. Marshall, presenting the Circuit Judges' Creed

Roujet DeLisle Marshall was born December 27, 1847, in Nashua, New Hampshire. In 1854, the Marshall family moved to a farm in Delton, Wisconsin. Marshall attended Lawrence College, but because of his father's failing health, Marshall's formal education was cut short so he could manage the family farm.

Marshall later studied law in Baraboo and served as justice of the peace. After admittance to the bar in 1873, Marshall formed a law partnership in Chippewa Falls. In 1876, Governor Harrison Ludington appointed Marshall judge for Chippewa County. A year later, Marshall was elected to a four-year term.

After leaving the bench, Marshall formed a new law partnership with John J. Jenkins, a former U.S. attorney for the Wyoming Territory. Marshall drafted many legislative bills for the lumber industry. It was said at Marshall's memorial that his success was attributed not to his personality, but to his profound understanding of the law. His professional and civic leadership was recognized by his appointment to the University of Wisconsin Board of Regents in 1884, where he served for five years.

Marshall was elected judge for the 11th Judicial Circuit in 1888 and was reelected in 1894. As circuit court judge in this rapidly growing district, Marshall was overworked. Almost every day he opened court at 8 A.M. and closed around 11:30 P.M. On one occasion, attorneys on both sides of several cases conspired to ask for continuances just to give the judge rest. He was moved to tears at their sensitivity.

Governor William H. Upham appointed the forty-eight-year-old Marshall to the Wisconsin Supreme Court in 1895, after the death of Chief Justice Harlow S. Orton. Marshall was elected to the office in 1897 and reelected in 1907. Although he was recognized as a fine jurist, he was known for having an easily flared temper. For instance, shortly before his reelection to the Supreme Court, he shouted angrily at a band playing the "Star Spangled Banner" in the capitol rotunda. While his actions may have cost him votes, it was not enough to lose an election.

In 1911, Marshall authored several opinions and other writings on personal injuries. The state legislature enacted the Workmen's Compensation Act the same year. It was said that Marshall's writing so closely resembled the "spirit and purpose" of the new law that it would be fair to say that Marshall, in part, was its origin.

It was told at Marshall's memorial service that a lawyer who knew Marshall well once said: "Judge Marshall never knew or understood the need of recreation; work seemed all-sufficient to him. At the opening of a term of court, one of the prominent attorneys was away for a week of fishing. Upon being told the reason for the absence, Judge Marshall said: 'I can't understand how a full-grown man can get any pleasure out of wasting his time fishing or hunting.'"

Marshall was also known for his especially long opinions, such as *Harrigan v. Gilchrist* (1904) which is 334 pages long and was described by Chief Justice John B. Winslow as a "compendium of legal lore."

After twenty-two years on the Supreme Court, Marshall stepped down in January 1918. He was married to Mary Jenkins; he died May 22, 1922.

Charles V. Bardeen
(1850–1903)
Wisconsin Supreme Court Justice
(1898–1903)

*"In his early youth he attended a session of this court, and upon his return home
from Madison expressed to his parents his determination and ambition to
become a member of the Supreme Court."*
—Marvin B. Rosenberry, Bardeen's memorial service (1903)

C harles Valdo Bardeen was born
September 23, 1850, in Brookfield,
New York. His family moved to a
farm in Wisconsin in 1854. Bardeen graduated
from high school in 1870. He worked in a law
firm and taught school in Edgerton for a year
until he received an urgent invitation from the
governor of Colorado, a former schoolmate, to
pursue a business venture in Colorado
Springs. Bardeen found a substitute teacher
and left immediately.

He returned to Wisconsin two years later
and graduated from the University of
Wisconsin Law School in 1875. He was in private law practice and served as city attorney
in Wausau for the next seventeen years. Active
in public affairs, Bardeen was superintendent
of public schools in Wausau and occasionally wrote for local newspapers.

Bardeen was elected judge for the newly created 16th Judicial Circuit in 1891
and served until his appointment to the Wisconsin Supreme Court in 1898.

At his memorial service, it was said that Bardeen was not considered a genius
but had common sense and a capacity and willingness for hard work. "His words,
whether written or spoken, always rang true. He had not the graces of the orator or
the poet, yet what he said or wrote was effective because it was sound and true,"
said Marvin B. Rosenberry, a Wausau attorney who later became a Wisconsin
Supreme Court chief justice.

Bardeen and his wife, Frances Miller, had three children: Eleanor, Charles, and
Florence. Bardeen died March 20, 1903, shortly before the end of his term on the
Supreme Court.

Joshua E. Dodge
(1854–1921)
Wisconsin Supreme Court Justice
(1898–1910)

"It fell to his lot to write the opinions in some of the most important decisions handed down by our Supreme Court, and his clear reasoning and literary eloquence did much to make this Supreme Court of Wisconsin respected and illustrious throughout the nation."
—Samuel M. Field, Dodge's memorial service (1921)

Joshua Eric Dodge was born October 25, 1854, in West Cambridge, Massachusetts. He was educated at Westford Academy in Massachusetts and later graduated from Iowa College (now Grinnell College). Dodge graduated from Boston University Law School in 1877.

Dodge came to Wisconsin and practiced law in Racine for fifteen years. He was a member of the state assembly from 1891 to 1892. In 1893, he was appointed to the Board of Commissioners for the Promotion of Uniformity of Legislation in the United States.

In September 1893, President Grover Cleveland appointed Dodge assistant U.S. attorney general. When the Cleveland administration left Washington, D.C., in 1897, Dodge returned to Milwaukee, where he practiced law.

After Justice Silas U. Pinney resigned from the Wisconsin Supreme Court in 1898, Dodge was appointed to fill the vacancy. His opinions are found in forty-three volumes of the *Wisconsin Reports*. His experience as a legislator added insight to the Supreme Court during a period marked by sweeping changes in statutory law.

Dodge was characterized by Samuel M. Field as a "gentleman of the old school." "He was a great teacher, patient, and always willing to explain his viewpoint and conclusions to the young lawyer who might seek his counsel," said Field at Dodge's memorial service.

Dodge retired from the Supreme Court after twelve years and resumed his law practice in Milwaukee. He was single and had no children. He died May 2, 1921.

Robert G. Siebecker
(1854–1922)

Wisconsin Supreme Court Justice
(1903–1922)

Chief Justice
(1920–1922)

*"There is romance in the career of this boy from the farm who closed his life
as the Chief Justice of this great court."*
—Judge E. Ray Stevens, Siebecker's memorial service (1923)

Robert George Siebecker was born in
Sauk County, Wisconsin, on October 17,
1854. His parents had emigrated from
Germany a few years earlier and settled on a
farm. At seventeen, Siebecker left the farm and
moved to Madison to attend the University of
Wisconsin. There he met his future wife,
Josephine La Follette.

After graduating from the University
of Wisconsin Law School in 1880, Siebecker
entered into a law partnership with his
brother-in-law, Robert M. La Follette (future
governor of Wisconsin and U.S. senator).
Siebecker practiced law until April 1886, when
he was elected city attorney for Madison. In
1890, Governor William D. Hoard appointed
him judge for the 9th Judicial Circuit.
Siebecker served in that position for the next thirteen years.

In April 1903, Siebecker was elected to the state Supreme Court for a term beginning in January 1904. However, shortly after his election the death of Justice Charles
V. Bardeen left a vacancy on the Supreme Court. Governor La Follette appointed
Siebecker to fill this seat. Siebecker was twice reelected to the Supreme Court and
became the chief justice upon the death of Chief Justice John B. Winslow in July 1920.

It was said at Siebecker's memorial that he was a kind and courteous circuit
court judge who "rendered thoughtful, well-reasoned decisions." As a justice,
Siebecker tackled tough constitutional issues on the subjects of taxation, insurance,
and regulation of public utilities.

An excellent speaker, Siebecker had a "fine presence and rich and pleasing
voice." He was often asked to address community groups. He loved nature and spent
his leisure time outdoors. He and his wife, Josephine, had four sons. Three sons survived them: Karl, Robert, and Lee. Siebecker died February 12, 1922.

James C. Kerwin

(1850–1921)

Wisconsin Supreme Court Justice

(1905–1921)

"His purposes of life were swayed by pure motives, his actions were guided by elevating principals of morality, and his conduct shows that he was an untiring warrior in defense of truth and the promotion of justice."
—Chief Justice Robert G. Siebecker, Kerwin's memorial service (1922)

James Charles Kerwin was born May 14, 1850, in Menasha, Wisconsin. He attended high school in Menasha and received his law degree from the University of Wisconsin Law School in 1875. After graduating, Kerwin practiced law in Neenah, where he served as city attorney for twelve years. He also maintained a law practice in Milwaukee until his obligations in Neenah became too time-consuming. Kerwin served as a member of the University of Wisconsin Board of Regents for three years.

In 1903, Kerwin was appointed to the Wisconsin Supreme Court. He declined the offer because of prior commitments to friends and clients. A year later, he was elected to the Wisconsin Supreme Court; he was reelected without opposition in 1914.

Chief Justice Robert G. Siebecker said of Kerwin's time on the Supreme Court: "He believed in and lived up to the principle that the administration of the law should be attended by a candid disclosure of everything involved in a dispute and that a trial in court should be a free and even contest for all the parties."

While on the Supreme Court, Kerwin was urged to accept an offer to be president of a large corporation, a position that have more than doubled his salary. According to a colleague, he never considered the proposal because he felt that "such action would tend to discredit the judiciary and undermine the confidence of the people in its integrity of purpose."

Throughout his professional career, including his sixteen years on the bench, Kerwin maintained his father's farm in Neenah. He kept it in operation until his death on January 29, 1921. Kerwin and his wife, Helen Lawson, had four daughters.

William H. Timlin

(1852–1916)

Wisconsin Supreme Court Justice

(1907–1916)

"His opinions disclose the man; they are logical, terse, clear, vigorous, and to the point. In some dissenting opinions the fire of combat glows—the spirit of the lawyer had not been wholly suppressed by the calm of the judicial mind."
—P. H. Martin, Timlin's memorial service (1917)

William Henry Timlin was born May 28, 1852, in Mequon, Wisconsin. His parents were Irish immigrants. When Timlin was six years old, his mother died. At the outbreak of the Civil War his father entered the army and disappeared while fighting. Timlin was sent to live with relatives, themselves struggling amid hardships. He worked on their farm and received little formal schooling.

When Timlin was a teenager, his uncle died, and Timlin had more years of hard labor, setbacks, and discouragement. Despite the difficulties, Timlin found time for independent study. He took up surveying, school teaching, and eventually stenography. At twenty-five, Timlin became the official stenographer of the Kewaunee County Circuit Court. In 1878, he was admitted to the bar and set up private law practice in Kewaunee County, where he also served as the superintendent of public schools.

Timlin later settled in Milwaukee and practiced law. His reputation as a successful and resourceful trial lawyer made him a promising candidate for the Wisconsin Supreme Court. Urged by his colleagues, he agreed to run in the election of 1906 and said: "No citizen has the right to refuse the obligation of public service when called upon."

Justice James C. Kerwin described Timlin as a "man of great wisdom, a scholar, pure in heart, patient, patriotic, impartial and courageous . . . [h]e was no phrase-maker, and never indulged in high-sounding platitudes for effect, but went straight to the point and avoided empty words."

Timlin and his wife, Cecelia Arpin, had four children. He died near the end of his Supreme Court term on August 21, 1916.

Robert M. Bashford

(1845–1911)

Wisconsin Supreme Court Justice

(1908)

*"His mind was strong, keen, and analytic. . . . He was a wise counselor
and loyal to his client. He was absolutely honest."*
—John A. Aylward, Bashford's memorial service (1911)

Robert McKee Bashford was born in Lafayette County, Wisconsin, on December 31, 1845. He and his three brothers spent much of their childhood working on the family farm. He graduated from the University of Wisconsin with a degree in ancient classical studies in 1870. He earned a law degree in 1871 and a master's degree in 1874.

In 1871, Bashford and two others purchased the *Democrat,* a Madison newspaper. In his capacity as editor, he influenced the successful gubernatorial campaigns of James R. Doolittle and William R. Taylor.

After leaving the paper, Bashford joined a Madison law firm and served as city attorney from 1881 to 1886. In 1886, he moved to Chicago to practice commercial and corporate law. The firm was successful in Chicago, but Bashford disliked the daily strain and returned to Madison.

In 1890, he was elected mayor of Madison and successfully assisted the state attorney general in prosecuting former state treasurers for the return of interest they had collected on the deposit of public funds. The state recovered nearly a half-million dollars.

Bashford was a state senator from 1893 to 1897, and he taught at the University of Wisconsin Law School for seven years. Bashford enjoyed working as a professor and having contact with young minds. "He gave them the best of himself and his spirit and the love of the law entered into many of his lectures," said John A. Aylward at Bashford's memorial service.

Bashford was appointed to the Wisconsin Supreme Court in January 1908, upon the death of Chief Justice John B. Cassoday. Six months after his appointment, he lost in a special election to John Barnes. At his memorial service, it was said that the election loss was a great disappointment to him, but he never complained, and he resumed his law practice. Bashford died January 29, 1911.

John Barnes
(1859–1919)
Wisconsin Supreme Court Justice
(1908–1916)

"He was gentle, unassuming, kind, and democratic; he had a fine sense of humor and indulged it with pleasure and to the delight of his companions. His nature was cordial, open, generous, yet marked by that quiet dignity and poise characteristic of big men."
—Patrick H. Martin, Barnes's memorial service (1919)

John Barnes was born July 26, 1859, and grew up on a farm in Manitowoc County, Wisconsin. Barnes graduated from high school in 1876 and continued his education at the Oshkosh Normal School. He taught school for the next six years.

After graduating from the University of Wisconsin Law School in 1885, Barnes returned to Oshkosh to practice law. In 1887, Barnes moved to Oneida County, where he practiced law and served as the municipal judge in Rhinelander for four years. He was president of the local school board, pursued many successful business ventures, and was a company executive.

Governor Robert M. La Follette appointed Barnes to the newly created Railroad Commission of Wisconsin in 1906. Barnes resigned after two and a half years on the commission. In 1908, Barnes was called back to public service. In a special election, he ran successfully for a Supreme Court seat against Robert M. Bashford, who had been appointed to fill the vacancy caused by Chief Justice John B. Cassoday's death. Barnes was elected to finish Cassoday's term; he won reelection to a ten-year term in 1909.

In 1916, Barnes resigned from the bench to become chief counsel for the Northwestern Mutual Life Insurance Company of Milwaukee. Barnes served in that capacity until his unexpected death on January 1, 1919, at age fifty-nine.

Barnes was married to Julia Koelzer, a childhood friend. They had four children: Beatrice, Fayne, Dorothy, and John.

Aad J. Vinje

(1857–1929)

Wisconsin Supreme Court Justice

(1910–1929)

Chief Justice

(1922–1929)

"There was nothing spectacular about Chief Justice Vinje so far as external appearances went, but he filled the position of chief justice with great honor, and he commanded the deep respect and veneration of all who knew this court in his day."
—John P. McGalloway, Wisconsin Supreme Court Centennial (1953)

Aad John Vinje was born in Voss, Norway, on November 10, 1857. He came to the United States with his parents when he was twelve years old. His family settled in Iowa, where he attended college and taught school for several years.

Vinje earned a law degree from the University of Wisconsin Law School in 1887. While in school, he worked in the State Law Library. After graduating in 1887, Vinje served as assistant Supreme Court reporter until 1891, when he moved to Superior, Wisconsin, to practice law.

In 1895, Vinje was appointed judge for the 11th Judicial Circuit. He served in that capacity until 1910, when he was appointed to the Wisconsin Supreme Court. He won election to ten-year terms in 1911 and 1921. Upon the death of Chief Justice Robert G. Siebecker in February 1922, Vinje became the chief justice, a position he occupied until his death on March 23, 1929.

At his memorial service, it was said that Vinje was a thoughtful, calm, impartial, and fearless justice. He listened with such attentiveness to arguments that those appearing before him were encouraged to do their very best. His opinions, which appear in fifty-four volumes of the *Wisconsin Reports,* are short, concise, logical, and convincing.

Off the bench, Vinje was known for his keen sense of humor and love of the outdoors. During his frequent wilderness excursions, he "completely laid aside the cloak of judicial dignity and joined in the merrymaking with the zest of a boy."

Vinje and his wife, Alice Miller, had four children: Arthur, David, Janet, and Ethel.

Marvin B. Rosenberry

(1868–1958)

Wisconsin Supreme Court Justice

(1916–1950)

Chief Justice

(1929–1950)

"Marvin B. Rosenberry is not only one of the most articulate spokesmen for democracy Wisconsin has ever seen, he is also one of the finest examples."
—*Wisconsin State Journal,* 1952

Marvin Bristol Rosenberry was born February 12, 1868, in Ohio and grew up on a farm in Michigan. Upon graduating from the University of Michigan Law School in 1893, he settled in Wausau, Wisconsin, and opened his own law office. He was a skilled lawyer and a vigorous advocate, even to the extent of defending himself physically on occasion.

Governor Emanuel L. Philipp appointed forty-eight-year-old Rosenberry to the state Supreme Court on February 12, 1916, to replace the resigning Justice John Barnes. In 1919, Rosenberry won election to a ten-year term. He won reelection in 1929 and 1939. Rosenberry became the chief justice in 1929 and served in that capacity for twenty-one years, longer than any other chief justice. In 1950, at age eighty-two, he retired from the Supreme Court.

During his thirty-four years on the bench, Rosenberry participated in approximately eleven thousand cases. His opinions span ninety-one volumes of the *Wisconsin Reports.* He believed that "justice delayed is justice denied" and seldom granted requests for postponement.

An avid outdoorsman, Rosenberry enjoyed hunting, fishing, and hiking. He was responsible for establishing miles of hiking trails in northern Wisconsin. He contributed much of his time and talents to the Boy Scouts of America, earning the highest awards given to adult scout leaders.

Rosenberry and his wife, Kate Landfair, had three children: Florence, Katherine, and Samuel. Rosenberry once brought his young son along to observe as he tried a case before the Wisconsin Supreme Court. On the train ride home, Rosenberry asked

Samuel what he thought of the oral argument. Samuel replied: "They holler a lot and pound the table."

Upon Kate's death, Rosenberry married Lois Matthews, dean of women and professor of history at the University of Wisconsin. Following his retirement from the bench, Rosenberry practiced law until a few weeks before his death at age ninety on February 15, 1958.

Franz C. Eschweiler
(1863–1929)
Wisconsin Supreme Court Justice
(1916–1929)

"His love for his fellow men and his love for justice were closely linked together, and he wanted to humanize the law."
—Justice Burr W. Jones, Eschweiler's memorial service (1929)

Franz Chadbourne Eschweiler was born September 6, 1863, in Houghton, Michigan. He attended college at the University of Michigan and the University of Iowa. In 1889, he was admitted to the bar in Milwaukee, where he practiced law for twenty-one years.

Eschweiler was appointed special prosecutor for Milwaukee County in 1907. Three years later, he was elected to Milwaukee County Circuit Court, where he served for six years. In 1912, he was chosen by his colleagues to preside in juvenile court. He once told a friend that the happiest moments of his official career were spent with children who had appeared before him while he was juvenile judge. He enjoyed giving advice and suggestions to help them rebuild their lives. Attorney S. C. Backus said of Eschweiler's work as juvenile judge: "He moved among these young men and women with a kind, gentle, yet dignified spirit, always with the thought of saving and assisting human souls."

Along with his work in juvenile court, Eschweiler taught at Marquette University Law School for twenty years. It was said at his memorial: "His considerate treatment and encouragement of his students, and his sincere parental interest in their welfare, in class and life after, resulted in many treasured friendships."

In 1916, Eschweiler was appointed to the Wisconsin Supreme Court. He received an honorary doctor of law degree from Marquette University in 1918. He was twice elected to the Supreme Court and served for thirteen years.

He was married to Ida Kindt and had four children: Elaine, John, Paul, and Mary. He died November 14, 1929.

Walter C. Owen
(1868–1934)
Wisconsin Supreme Court Justice
(1918–1934)

"He was always kind, considerate, open-minded, tolerant. The attachments which he formed were lasting and deep. While upon every occasion he supported his views firmly and skillfully, he was always willing to reconsider his opinion and to give respectful and sympathetic hearing to those who opposed him."
—Chief Justice Marvin B. Rosenberry, Owen's memorial service (1934)

Walter Cecil Owen was born September 26, 1868, near Trenton Prairie, Wisconsin. He attended high school and common school before earning a teaching certificate. He taught in a rural school for a few years and later served as principal of Maiden Rock Village School. In addition to teaching, Owen studied law to prepare for the University of Wisconsin Law School, where he received his degree in 1891.

After graduating, Owen moved to Superior, where he and childhood friends William R. Foley and Charles H. Crownhart (later a state Supreme Court justice) started a law firm. When the economy in Superior suffered from the depression of the 1890s, Owen returned to Maiden Rock to practice law.

Owen's career in public service began when he was first elected to the state senate in 1906 and continued until his death. During his two terms as senator, major legislation was enacted, including the Workmen's Compensation Act (written in part by Crownhart), the Income Tax Act, and the State Highway Act.

In 1912, Owen won his first of three elections for attorney general of Wisconsin. He was known as an excellent administrator. His office released more than two thousand official opinions over a five-year period. The "clear, concise, direct, and simple elegant language" that characterized his legal writing as attorney general made him a fine choice for the vacant seat on the Wisconsin Supreme Court. He was elected in 1917. He resigned as attorney general in 1918 and began serving on the Supreme Court; later he was reelected to the Supreme Court for a second term without opposition.

Attorney Ferris M. White said of Owen: "He was at once attentive and impartial, considerate of the young lawyers and patient with the old. He was never swayed from the true judicial attitude."

Owen became ill in 1933. At the urging of his friends and colleagues on the bench, he retreated to Florida to recover. When his health improved, he made plans to return to Wisconsin to resume his duties on the bench. On the eve of his departure, he suffered a relapse; he died April 15, 1934. He was married to Alta Otis and had one daughter, Laures Margaret.

Burr W. Jones

(1846–1935)

Wisconsin Supreme Court Justice

(1920–1926)

"Justice Jones was one of the noblest and most useful citizens this state ever produced.
He was without conceit. He was genuine. He had a capacity for friendships."

—Judge Evan A. Evans, Jones's memorial service (1935)

Burr W. Jones was born March 9, 1846, in Evansville, Wisconsin. He lived and worked on a farm and was educated at the Evansville Seminary. Jones was encouraged early on, even by his first grade teacher, to pursue a career in law. Jones saved money for college by teaching for two years. When he enrolled at the University of Wisconsin, there were 250 students, and room and board cost $1.25 per week.

After graduating from the University of Wisconsin Law School in 1871, Jones entered the Madison law office of Col. Wiliam F. Vilas (later a U.S. senator). Jones was elected district attorney of Dane County in 1872 and was reelected in 1874.

After a single U.S. congressional term in 1882, Jones worked as a professor at the University of Wisconsin Law School for thirty years. At the same time, he returned to private law practice at the office of Lamb & Jones. Jones later formed a partnership with E. Ray Stevens.

Jones served as chair of the state Democratic Convention in 1892. In 1896, he published a three-volume treatise, *Jones on Evidence,* which was followed by several editions. He was appointed to the first Wisconsin Tax Commission in 1897 and was later elected chair. Jones served as president of the State Bar Association in 1906.

In 1920, upon the death of Chief Justice John B. Winslow, Governor Emanual L. Philipp appointed Jones to the Wisconsin Supreme Court. He was elected to the court in 1922. As he was nearing eighty years old, he chose not to seek reelection and was succeeded by his former law partner, E. Ray Stevens.

Jones was married to Olive Hoyt. They had one daughter, Marion. After Olive died, Jones married Katherine MacDonald. He died January 7, 1935.

Christian Doerfler
(1862–1934)
Wisconsin Supreme Court Justice
(1921–1929)

*"There is no human attribute over and above goodness. Mr. Doerfler was a good man. . . .
He abhorred hypocrisy. In the sense of goodness, righteousness, and integrity,
he was truly a noble man."*
—Benjamin Poss, Doerfler's memorial service (1936)

Christian Doerfler was born March 2, 1862, in Milwaukee. After attending the Milwaukee Normal School, he spent three years teaching. Doerfler graduated from the University of Wisconsin Law School in 1885. He served as commissioner for the Milwaukee Public Schools and assistant district attorney of Milwaukee County from 1889 to 1891.

An active Republican who identified with the progressive La Follette movement, Doerfler was a delegate to several Republican National Conventions. He served as president of the Milwaukee County Bar Association and the Wisconsin State Bar from 1914 to 1915.

Doerfler was frequently asked to speak on public welfare. "He was tolerant—liberal in thought. The oppressed, whatever their race or religion and wheresoever their abode, found hope and promise of renewed living as he championed their cause and labored for their betterment," said Benjamin Poss at Doerfler's memorial service.

In 1921, Governor John J. Blaine appointed Doerfler to succeed the late Justice James C. Kerwin on the Wisconsin Supreme Court. Doerfler ran unopposed for election in 1924. Ill health forced him to resign from the Supreme Court in 1929. He spent his retirement reading, traveling, and working in his flower garden at his home in Milwaukee.

Doerfler was married to Julia Anderson. They had one son, Fredric, who died in 1923 while a student at the University of Wisconsin. Doerfler died June 10, 1934.

Charles H. Crownhart
(1863–1930)
Wisconsin Supreme Court Justice
(1922–1930)

"In Crownhart's own words, he believed that the trend of government 'has been to secure more freedom, a greater security of property and person, more education, more of the comforts of life and the preservation of the rights of conscience.'"
—Edward J. Dempsey, Crownhart's memorial service (1930)

Charles Henry Crownhart was born April 16, 1863, in New Castle, Wisconsin. He graduated from River Falls Normal School in 1886 and received a law degree from the University of Wisconsin Law School in 1889.

In 1891, Crownhart moved to Superior to start a law firm with Walter C. Owen (who later became a Wisconsin Supreme Court justice). While practicing law for twenty years, Crownhart served as Douglas County district attorney and was a member of the Board of Regents of Normal Schools.

Crownhart was the principal draftsman of the first Workmen's Compensation Act enacted in Wisconsin in 1911. Prior to this legislation, there was no statutory compensation for work-related injuries, and claims for damages for such injuries flooded the courts. Crownhart was then appointed chair of Wisconsin's first Industrial Commission, where he worked with John R. Commons and Joseph D. Beck.

Crownhart, a close friend and advisor to U.S. Senator Robert M. La Follette, was active in the Wisconsin Progressive movement. In 1910, Crownhart managed La Follette's first congressional campaign.

In 1921, the state Supreme Court appointed Crownhart the reviser of statutes. A year later, Governor John J. Blaine appointed him to the court, and he won election soon after.

The Dane County Bar said of Crownhart: "He was no believer of a cloistered judiciary. He saw the judiciary as but an agency of democracy, an agency that must be ever in touch with the people and with the progress of human institutions, to perform aright its functions."

Crownhart and his wife, Jessie Evans, had two sons, Jesse and Charles. Crownhart died on May 2, 1930.

E. Ray Stevens

(1869–1930)

Wisconsin Supreme Court Justice

(1926–1930)

"He was a slave to his work, but a willing slave, and like most happy men
he really loved his work."
—Justice Burr W. Jones, Stevens's memorial service (1930)

Edmund Ray Stevens was born June 20, 1869, in Lake County, Illinois, and his family later settled in Janesville, Wisconsin. He received a law degree from the University of Wisconsin in 1895 and entered the law office of Burr W. Jones (later a Supreme Court justice). A year later, they established the firm Jones & Stevens, which operated until 1903.

In 1901, Stevens was elected to the state assembly, where he helped shape the state's primary election system. In 1903, Governor Robert M. La Follette appointed the thirty-four-year-old Stevens judge for the 9th Judicial Circuit. As a judge, Stevens became an authority on reviewing the decisions of various state commissions that regulated tax collection, transportation systems, and employer/employee relations.

While on the bench, Stevens lectured at the University of Wisconsin Law School for five years and was active at the Wisconsin Historical Society. Stevens was a circuit court judge until his election to the Wisconsin Supreme Court in 1926, where he served until his death in 1930.

Known for his untiring devotion to his job, Stevens participated in more than 1,700 cases and wrote 237 opinions in his four years on the Supreme Court. "He crowded into his sixty-one years of life more of usefulness than most men even of high ability, in fourscore years can contribute to their fellowmen, " said Burr W. Jones at Stevens's memorial service.

Stevens was not interested in hunting, fishing, golf, nor cards, which many of his friends enjoyed, but he loved nature. Although his career did not allow for much leisure time, he enjoyed hiking, gardening, and taking cruises on Lake Michigan.

Stevens was married to Kate Sabin. They had two sons, Myron and Henry. Myron practiced law in Madison for many years and was a partner in the firm of Ross & Stevens.

Chester A. Fowler
(1862–1948)
Wisconsin Supreme Court Justice
(1929–1948)

"An unsuspected sense of humor, a vast capacity of work, a broad experience at the bar and on the bench, an intuitive sense of what the law should be, together with a complete willingness to search the facts and the books for the right rule always characterized him."
—John P. McGalloway, Wisconsin Supreme Court Centennial (1953)

Chester Almeron Fowler was born Christmas Eve 1862, in Rubicon, Wisconsin. His father was a soldier in the Union Army during the Civil War. After graduating from Whitewater Normal School in 1884, Fowler served one year as a grade school principal and two years as a high school principal.

Fowler graduated from the University of Wisconsin in 1887 and studied law at a private firm in West Union, Iowa. He practiced law in Omaha, Nebraska, from 1889 to 1894. In November 1894, he and his law partner returned to Wisconsin and opened law offices in Portage and Montello. They owned one of the best private law libraries in the state. While in Portage, Fowler held the office of city attorney for six years. He also became an avid curler, a sport he enjoyed until the age of eighty.

Fowler was elected judge to the newly created 18th Judicial Circuit in 1905. He was chair of the Board of Circuit Judges for ten years. He ran unsuccessfully for the Wisconsin Supreme Court in 1916. He was appointed to the Supreme Court in 1929, upon the death of Chief Justice Aad J. Vinje, and won election in 1931 and reelection in 1941.

While on the Supreme Court, Fowler wrote 862 majority, 85 dissenting, and 6 concurring opinions. His sharp criticism of the use of "and/or" in *Employers Mutual Life Insurance Co. v. Tollefsen* (1935) immediately received national attention and is still quoted and referred to in both professional and lay publications.

Fowler died on April 8, 1948. He was married to Carrie Julia Smith. They had twins, Dwight and Mary.

Oscar M. Fritz
(1878–1957)
Wisconsin Supreme Court Justice
(1929–1954)
Chief Justice
(1950–1954)

*"His every action as a judge was motivated by conscientious devotion to duty. . . .
His opinions, with their accurate and often lengthy detailed statement of the facts,
bear witness to this industry."*
—Justice George R. Currie, Fritz's memorial service (1957)

Oscar Marion Fritz was born March 3, 1878, in Milwaukee. His father, Theodore Fritz, was a state senator. The Fritz family lived in Milwaukee for more than fifty-five years. Fritz graduated from a Milwaukee public high school and attended what is now Marquette University Law School. He received his law degree from the University of Wisconsin Law School in 1901.

Fritz practiced law from 1901 to 1912, when he was appointed a circuit judge for Milwaukee County. He served in that role for seventeen years and was chair of the Wisconsin Board of Circuit Judges for six years.

In 1929, Fritz was appointed to the Wisconsin Supreme Court. Justice Edward T. Fairchild commended Fritz's opinion in *School District v. Callahan* (1941) as an influential and well-researched work. The case addressed reorganization of school district administration and the constitutional and statutory provisions regarding public instruction.

Fritz became the chief justice in 1950. He retired in 1954, just one year before his term expired. He had spent forty-two years in the judiciary, more than twenty-four of them on the Wisconsin Supreme Court.

During retirement, Fritz enjoyed gardening, reading, and traveling throughout the United States. He was married to Ena Lorch, and they had two children. Ena died in 1945, and Fritz later married Anna Marie Millmann. He died October 5, 1957.

Edward T. Fairchild
(1872–1965)
Wisconsin Supreme Court Justice
(1930–1957)
Chief Justice
(1954–1957)

"All you have to do is to use common sense, the trouble starts when you have to decide whose common sense is to prevail."
—Chief Justice Edward T. Fairchild, oral history (1957)

Edward Thomas Fairchild was born June 17, 1872, in Towanda, Pennsylvania. He was raised and educated in Dansville, New York. He was admitted to the New York Bar in 1894 and was the last Wisconsin Supreme Court justice not to earn a law degree from an institution of higher learning. Although he spent the majority of his life in Wisconsin, he never lost the connection with his hometown. He bought a farm in Dansville in the 1920s and returned to vacation there throughout his life.

Fairchild moved to Milwaukee in 1897 and practiced law there for nineteen years. From 1903 to 1906, he was an assistant district attorney for Milwaukee County. He was elected to the Wisconsin senate in 1906 and served for two sessions. In 1910, he ran unsuccessfully for governor of Wisconsin, and he was reelected to the senate in 1914.

Fairchild was appointed a circuit judge for Milwaukee County in 1916, where he served until his appointment to the Wisconsin Supreme Court in 1930. Fairchild's chambers served as the "social center of the court." Fellow justices gathered there to have tea and tell stories. A skillful storyteller, Fairchild often entertained his company with amusing accounts of political and legal battles from the turn of the century.

Fairchild became chief justice in 1954. After forty years of service in the state judiciary, he retired from the Supreme Court in 1957 at age eighty-four. Before retiring, Fairchild swore in his son, Thomas E. Fairchild, as a member of the Wisconsin Supreme Court.

Fairchild helped people throughout his life. He was active in organizing Milwaukee's Community Welfare Council and the Urban League of Milwaukee. While in the senate, he introduced legislation supporting vocational training and later became known as the "father of the vocational school system in Wisconsin." He also served on a committee that wrote the Workmen's Compensation Act.

Fairchild was married to Helen McCurdy Edwards. Two of their five children, Anne and Thomas, survived him upon his death at age ninety-three on October 29, 1965.

John D. Wickhem
(1888–1949)
Wisconsin Supreme Court Justice
(1930–1949)

"Wickhem was a deadpan humorist. One story he told was that after he won election to the court, a family friend congratulated him on winning election to the court (equivalent to today's municipal courts). Wickhem quietly corrected him, saying it was the Supreme Court. The friend said, 'Oh that's all right. Someday you'll get to the Superior Court.'"
—remarks by Judge Thomas E. Fairchild (1998)

John Dunne Wickhem was born in Beloit, Wisconsin, on May 25, 1888. He graduated from Beloit College in 1910 and remained in Beloit as a high school teacher and athletic coach until 1914, when he entered the University of Wisconsin Law School. He graduated in two years by attending summer sessions. Upon graduation, he worked at the law office of Attorney Burr W. Jones (later a state Supreme Court justice). Wickhem left Madison in 1917 and joined a Milwaukee law firm.

During World War I, Wickhem worked in the War Trade Intelligence Bureau in Washington, D.C. Returning to Wisconsin in 1919, he was appointed an assistant professor at the University of Wisconsin Law School. He became a full professor in 1925 and remained on the faculty until his appointment to the Wisconsin Supreme Court on September 25, 1930. Wickhem won election to the bench in 1933 and 1943.

He wrote the opinion in *State ex rel Martin v. Heil* (1942), which decided the succession as governor when Governor-Elect Orland S. Loomis died before taking office. It was decided that the sitting governor, Julius P. Heil, would not continue in office, but that Lieutenant-Governor Walter S. Goodland would serve out Loomis's term.

Wickhem's opinions were described as "excellent examples of legal reasoning and clarity of expression." Wickhem said that he became a student of the law in 1914 and remained so for life. He once said that his greatest satisfaction came from "digging into a tough legal decision."

A brilliant conversationalist and an accomplished speaker, Wickhem was also described as a "flashy dresser." He was a calm, objective, patient, and understanding teacher and counselor. At his memorial service, his colleagues on the bench spoke of his equable temperament and balanced personality.

Wickhem and his wife, Mary Luella Carroll, had two sons, John and Robert. John was admitted to the bar a few months before his father's death on June 19, 1949.

George B. Nelson
(1876–1943)
Wisconsin Supreme Court Justice
(1930–1942)

"Not only was Judge Nelson active in his profession, but he was untiring in his devotion to matters of public concern and public welfare in his community and state."
—Theodore W. Brazeau, Nelson's memorial service (1943)

George Bliss Nelson was born May 21, 1876, in Amherst, Wisconsin. He attended the University of Wisconsin and was a member of the Philomathian Debating Society. He often said it was debating that laid the foundation for his legal career. He earned a law degree from George Washington Law School in 1902. While in Washington, D.C., Nelson spent his free time listening to discussions on the floor of Congress.

After law school, Nelson returned to Stevens Point to practice law. In 1906, he was appointed district attorney of Portage County, a seat he held until 1913. He served one term as city attorney for Stevens Point. Considered a strong trial lawyer, he was the lead prosecutor in *Lasecki v. State*, a high-profile murder trial in 1926. It was said at Nelson's memorial service that his work on this case will be forever

known as a "fine example of conscientious and thorough work in criminal prosecution."

During World War I, Nelson was active in civic organizations such as the Red Cross, Liberty Loan drives, and the YMCA. He was deeply religious and held leadership roles in the Episcopal church for thirty years.

In 1930, Governor Walter J. Kohler, Sr., appointed Nelson to the Wisconsin Supreme Court. The early years of his tenure were during the Great Depression. The Supreme Court grappled with many problems arising out of the economic disorder and the efforts of the government to alleviate the situation.

In 1940, Nelson became ill and was unable to attend court. He resigned in December 1942. His resignation letter read in part: "Until quite recently, I had the strong expectation of being able to return to my work on the Supreme Court. That now seems to be out of the question, at least for some time."

Nelson and his wife, Ruth Weller, had four children: Elizabeth, James II, Reginald, and George, Jr. Nelson died January 10, 1943.

Theodore G. Lewis
(1890–1934)
Wisconsin Supreme Court Justice
(1934)

The justice who never heard a case.

"The life of 'Ted' Lewis, from country boy to the Supreme Court, should forever keep aglow the cherished American tradition that determination, effort, and honest devotion to one's chosen field, lead with certainty to the most cherished of all our rewards—the fullness and enjoyment of life. . . ."
—William R. Curkeet, Lewis's memorial service (1936)

Theodore Gorman Lewis was born on a farm in McFarland, Wisconsin, on November 19, 1890. He graduated from Cambridge High School in 1909 and attended business college in Madison. Lewis received a bachelor's degree from the University of Wisconsin in 1913 and a law degree two years later. He was admitted to the bar and joined a Madison law firm.

During World War I, Lewis enrolled in Officer Training Camp at Fort Sheridan, Illinois. He was commissioned second lieutenant in August 1917 and was promoted to first lieutenant later that year. He was active in the 32nd division in Europe until he was wounded in a battle in France. After recovering, Lewis served with the Army of Occupation in Germany. He was honorably discharged in June 1919 and was awarded the Purple Heart for his distinguished service.

Lewis returned to Madison and resumed law practice, but he remained active in military affairs. From 1921 to 1925, he served as district attorney for Dane County and was elected to two terms as city attorney in the early 1930s. In 1933, Lewis was named executive secretary to Governor Albert G. Schmedeman (who had been the mayor of Madison when Lewis was the city attorney). Public confidence in Lewis helped smooth problems facing the executive office during this period.

On November 15, 1934, Schmedeman appointed the forty-three-year-old Lewis to the Wisconsin Supreme Court to fill the vacancy caused by the death of Justice Walter C. Owen. Lewis died of pneumonia twenty days later, on December 5, 1934, never having heard a case.

Lewis was married to Mabel Davidson Inbusch. They had two children, Nancy and Theodore, Jr.

Joseph Martin
(1878–1946)
Wisconsin Supreme Court Justice
(1934–1946)

"He was a powerful and most interesting speaker on political questions, having spoken in almost every county in the state of Wisconsin, and whether there were seven or eight people or whether there were thousands, his talk was delivered in the same vigor and seriousness."
—G. F. Clifford, Martin's memorial service (1947)

Joseph Martin was born May 12, 1878, in Rockland, Wisconsin. He graduated from West De Pere High School in 1897 and attended the University of Wisconsin Law School but never graduated. His brothers, who were lawyers, helped him prepare for the bar exam, which he passed in 1903. From 1903 to 1904, Martin served in the Wisconsin assembly; he later became a partner in his brothers' law firm in Green Bay.

Martin took an active interest in civic affairs on both the local and state level. He was a longtime member of the Green Bay School Board and the Elks and Lions Clubs. Prior to his appointment to the bench, he was active in the Democratic Party and served as the state party head.

Martin was a respected trial lawyer. He forged ties with his clients both professionally and socially. He thought of his law practice not as a money-driven business, but as a way to help people, and he often provided his services free of charge. G. F. Clifford said of Martin: "It was hard for many of his friends, after he became a member of the Supreme Court, to refuse to take their problems to him. He still was their friend and counselor, and while he had to inform them that he could not advise them on legal matters, he still had his office swarming with people who wanted to come in to talk things over."

Martin was appointed to the Wisconsin Supreme Court in 1934 by Governor Albert G. Schmedeman, a close friend. He accepted the appointment hesitantly, worried that he could not adopt the temperament necessary for impartial judicial decision-making and abandon his many years as a partisan, aggressive trial lawyer. Although he expected criticism of his appointment, he was surprised to find that those who questioned his ability became supporters when he successfully sought election in 1937.

It was said that Martin's strength on the Supreme Court was not opinion writing, but his deep understanding of human nature. He served until his death on March 19, 1946, at age sixty-seven. He and his wife, Mildred Wright, had four children.

Elmer E. Barlow
(1887–1948)
Wisconsin Supreme Court Justice
(1942–1948)

"To his wide knowledge of the law and of its application to practical affairs he added a sympathetic understanding of the background out of which controversies arose, and foresaw the effect of the court's decision upon the life of the parties and the public."
—Chief Justice Marvin B. Rosenberry, Barlow's memorial service (1948)

E lmer Elbert Barlow was born May 18, 1887, on a small farm in Arcadia, Wisconsin. Barlow attended the University of Wisconsin and played catcher for the UW baseball team, which toured Japan in 1909. When Barlow graduated from law school in 1909, he turned down offers to become a professional baseball player to pursue a career in law.

Barlow practiced law in La Crosse until 1939, when he was appointed executive counsel to Governor Julius P. Heil. A short time later, Heil appointed Barlow state tax commissioner. Barlow was known for reorganizing and efficiently administrating the tax department.

Although he had no previous judicial experience, Barlow was appointed to the Wisconsin Supreme Court in 1942. Barlow won election to the Supreme Court in 1945, beating Secretary of State Fred Zimmerman, a great voter-getter but a non-lawyer.

Chief Justice Marvin B. Rosenberry said of Barlow's work on the Supreme Court: "When Judge Barlow spoke for the court he carefully and accurately reflected his view that the opinion of the court is the composite of the contributions of each of its members. His judgment and understanding made his exposition of the problems in a particular case a genuine contribution to the decision."

Barlow was active at the University of Wisconsin. He served on the Athletic Board, was a director of the University of Wisconsin Foundation, and was president of the Law School Alumni Association.

Barlow was married to Kate Clausen. They had two children, Elizabeth and Robert. Kate died in 1930, and Barlow married Anna Wohlgenant in 1937. He died unexpectedly of a heart attack on June 26, 1948.

James Ward Rector
(1903–1979)
Wisconsin Supreme Court Justice
(1946–1947)

"He possessed in rare degree the judicial qualities of integrity, the capacity to suspend judgment, fairness, wide learning, broad experience, industry and concern for people and their problems."
—Robert B. L. Murphy, Rector's memorial service (1982)

James Ward Rector was born in Glenwood, Missouri, on June 24, 1903. Although he occasionally skipped school to attend trials in the local courthouse, he graduated from high school at the age of sixteen. He attended the University of Missouri but left during the farm depression of 1921 to earn money for school by working in the logging industry.

Rector enrolled in the University of Wisconsin in 1925, at the urging of Glenn Frank, the president of the university and a friend of the Rector family. Rector lived with the Frank family and tutored Frank's son.

Rector graduated from law school in 1930 and joined a Madison law firm. His impressive career included service as executive secretary to Governor Albert G. Schmedeman, special counsel to Governor Julius P. Heil, and deputy attorney general for the state. While working in the Office of the

Attorney General, he argued and won fourteen cases before the Wisconsin Supreme Court.

Rector was appointed to the Wisconsin Supreme Court in April 1946 to fill the vacancy created by Justice Joseph Martin's death. Rector ran for a full term in 1947 but was defeated. He ran and was defeated again in 1949. At Rector's memorial service, his son said that although his father was deeply hurt by his election losses, he never expressed bitterness.

After leaving the Supreme Court in 1947, Rector was offered a post as a judge in the Nuremberg war crimes trials. He declined, stating that the proceedings did not further the cause of law no matter how much the defendants might have deserved the punishments they were to receive.

Rector was appointed chief counsel to the Public Service Commission in 1948. He resigned in 1949 and became vice president of First Wisconsin Trust Company of Milwaukee, a position he held until he retired in 1968. Rector maintained a working relationship with a Milwaukee law firm until his death.

Rector and his wife, Virginia, had four children: James, Jr. (who served as a Wisconsin Supreme Court commissioner), Schuyler, Nancy, and Kathleen. Rector died August 6, 1979, at age seventy-six.

Henry P. Hughes
(1904–1968)
Wisconsin Supreme Court Justice
(1948–1951)

"As a trial judge, he was quick to come to the point. He could intersperse his official judicial language with what he really wanted to say."
—Charles F. Nolan, Hughes's portrait hanging (1973)

Henry P. Hughes was born August 13, 1904, in Fountain Prairie, Wisconsin. He graduated from St. Peter's High School and continued his education at Marquette University. In 1927, Hughes graduated from Georgetown University Law School, passed the Wisconsin Bar, and joined a law firm in Oshkosh.

In the early 1930s, Hughes was appointed and later elected Oshkosh city attorney and municipal judge. In 1937, Governor Phillip F. La Follette appointed him circuit judge for Winnebago County, where he served for ten years.

In 1946, Hughes ran unsuccessfully for the Wisconsin Supreme Court against Edward T. Fairchild. A year later, he ran again and won by more than 135,000 votes.

After three years on the bench, Hughes resigned and resumed his law practice in Oshkosh. He said that the justice's salary of $10,000 a year was insufficient to educate his children. His only departure from the law was in 1957, when he unsuccessfully sought the Republican nomination for the office of U.S. senator. Former Governor Walter J. Kohler, Jr., won the nomination but was defeated in the election by William Proxmire.

On December 12, 1968, on his way home from the memorial service for former Chief Justice John E. Martin, Hughes was killed when his car crashed into the back of a school bus. Hughes and his wife, Dorothy, had four sons: Patrick, James, Thomas, and Robert.

John E. Martin
(1891–1968)
Wisconsin Supreme Court Justice
(1948–1962)
Chief Justice
(1957–1962)

"Martin was a solid lawyer, shrewd, wise in the way of humanity, with a rare gift of earthy common sense. . . . He was a man full of humor and fun as well as accomplishment."
—Editorial, *Milwaukee Journal* (1968)

John E. Martin was born in Green Bay, Wisconsin, on November 15, 1891. He graduated from East High School in Green Bay and attended both the University of Wisconsin and Marquette University. He graduated from Notre Dame Law School in 1916.

Martin enlisted in the U.S. Army in August 1917 and became a lieutenant after attending Officer Training Camp at Fort Sheridan. While overseas, he fought alongside Theodore G. Lewis, Edward J. Gehl, and Roland J. Steinle, all of whom became Wisconsin Supreme Court justices. Martin was wounded and was awarded the

Purple Heart. He was honorably discharged as a captain in 1921.

Martin returned to Green Bay and practiced law with his father, Patrick, and his uncle, Joseph, who also became a member of the state Supreme Court. Martin moved to Milwaukee and was appointed assistant district attorney in 1933.

In 1938, Martin was part of the Republican-Democratic coalition with the goal of defeating the Progressives. He was elected attorney general for Wisconsin and was reelected to four two-year terms thereafter. A colleague on the Supreme Court recalled that while Martin was attorney general, he visited a northern Wisconsin town. When his group stopped at a local tavern, Martin asked the bartender where the (illegal) slot machines were. The bartender replied, "We had to put them away. The Big Guy is in town." He was referring to the attorney general, of course, but did not recognize Martin.

Governor Oscar Rennebohm appointed Martin to the Wisconsin Supreme Court in 1948. Martin was elected in 1950 and became chief justice in January 1957, when Chief Justice Edward T. Fairchild retired. In 1961, Martin was the first Wisconsinite to serve as chair of the National Conference of Chief Justices.

Martin retired from the Supreme Court in January 1962 and was appointed the first court administrator of Wisconsin. Because of his failing health, Martin retired in 1967.

Martin and his wife, Mary Kerwin, had two children, John and Mary Hope. He died December 9, 1968.

Grover L. Broadfoot
(1892–1962)
Wisconsin Supreme Court Justice
(1948–1962)
Chief Justice
(1962)

"His genuine humility was the kind, not that underrates one's self, but that is not puffed up and sees good in others wherever it may be found. The Wisconsin community is richer for the likes of Grover Broadfoot. Such men are rare."
—Editorial, *Milwaukee Journal* (1962)

Grover L. Broadfoot was born December 27, 1892, in Independence, Wisconsin. His family later settled in Mondovi. He attended the University of Wisconsin, paying for school by working as a hotel bellhop and later as an editorial assistant at a Madison newspaper. He was editor-in-chief of the university yearbook, the *Badger*. Broadfoot earned a law degree from the University of Wisconsin in 1918 but did not practice law until he completed service in the U.S. Army during World War I.

After the war, Broadfoot became active in public service. He was the Buffalo County district attorney for twelve years, Mondovi city attorney for twenty years, and mayor of Mondovi for four years. He was also president of Mondovi State Bank. After Broadfoot became a justice, he loved to return to Mondovi in the summers. In poker games in Buffalo County, he was known as "Old Stoneface."

Broadfoot was appointed to the Wisconsin Board of Tax Appeals in 1939 but resigned in 1943. A year later, he was elected to the Wisconsin legislature. He served in the legislature until his appointment as Wisconsin attorney general in 1948. He lost the primary election for attorney general later that year but was appointed to the Wisconsin Supreme Court in November 1948. He was elected to the Supreme Court in 1952 and reelected in 1955.

Broadfoot's colleagues on the Supreme Court noted that two of his greatest contributions in conference were his "prodigious memory" and his ability to act as peacemaker. He often recalled past decisions of the Supreme Court, relevant to the situation at hand, that had escaped the attention of the other justices.

Broadfoot became chief justice in January 1962. On May 3, 1962, decision day, Broadfoot revealed that his vision was so impaired that he was unable to read the mandate in a case in which he had written the opinion. He left the bench and never returned. He died May 18 of that year. He and his wife, Margaret Jacobi, had one son, John.

Timothy Brown
(1889–1977)
Wisconsin Supreme Court Justice
(1949–1964)
Chief Justice
(1962–1964)

"Timothy Brown was a great man with many laudable interests and accomplishments in many fields. His activities in sailing, literature, and public and civic service are legend in this community."
—Chief Justice Bruce F. Beilfuss, Brown's memorial service (1977)

Timothy Brown was born February 24, 1889, and raised in Madison. He earned a bachelor's degree at the University of Wisconsin in 1911 and graduated from Harvard Law School in 1914. He returned to Wisconsin and practiced law in Milwaukee for two years.

During World War I, Brown joined the U.S. Navy as a seaman and served on a destroyer overseas. As a boy he had sailed on Lake Mendota, and he chose the navy because of his lifelong love of sailing. After discharge from the navy, Brown returned to Madison to practice law. He served as a Dane County court commissioner until 1949 and also as executive counsel to Governors Walter S. Goodland and Oscar Rennebohm.

In 1949, Brown filled three months on the Wisconsin Public Service Commission and was then appointed to the Wisconsin Supreme Court. Brown became the chief justice in May 1962, upon the death of Chief Justice Grover L. Broadfoot.

According to a colleague, Brown had a "pixy-like" quality about him and was "full of fun." As chief justice, Brown requested that the tall, stiff ceremonial chairs behind the bench in the Hearing Room be replaced with comfortable chairs during oral argument. A colleague noted that when the salesperson brought sample chairs for the justices to try out, Brown, who was rather short, sat in one that he liked and commented that it was the first time as a justice that his feet were able to touch the floor.

During his tenure on the Supreme Court, Brown figured prominently in a decision that declared a state law that forced children to pay child support for their parents to be unconstitutional. Brown is also known for his role in overturning a lower court ruling that unions could be prohibited from picketing.

Brown retired at the end of his term in January 1964. In addition to being an active alumnus at the University of Wisconsin, Brown was a longtime officer of the Wisconsin Alumni Research Foundation, which he cofounded.

Brown's wife, Margaret Titchener, died in 1936. They had one son, Timothy, Jr. Brown later married Louise Coxon. He died December 31, 1977.

Edward J. Gehl
(1890–1956)
Wisconsin Supreme Court Justice
(1950–1956)

"It may be said that he was as gentle as spring, loving as summer, bounteous as autumn, and yet when occasion demanded, as stern and severe as the blighted frosts of bleak December."
—Justice Roland J. Steinle, Gehl's memorial service (1957)

E dward John Gehl was born January 26, 1890, in Hartford, Wisconsin. He graduated from Hartford High School in 1908 and received a law degree from the University of Wisconsin Law School in 1913. Gehl was in private practice until 1917, when he volunteered to serve in the U.S. Army during World War I. There he became close friends with three other men who also became Wisconsin Supreme Court justices: Roland J. Steinle, John E. Martin, and Theodore G. Lewis. Gehl was promoted to the rank of captain and was also awarded the Purple Heart and the Silver Star. Upon discharge, he continued service in the National Guard, where he rose to the rank of lieutenant colonel.

Following the war, Gehl practiced law in Hartford until 1932 and then served for two years as U.S. district attorney for the Eastern District of Wisconsin. He was elected judge to the 13th Judicial Circuit in 1940. In 1947, he served as chair of the Wisconsin Board of Circuit Judges.

Gehl was elected to the Wisconsin Supreme Court in 1949. He was the first justice elected under a 1949 law that ensured that the winner must receive a majority of the votes cast. He was well respected by his colleagues. Governor Walter J. Kohler, Jr., said of Gehl's work on the bench: "Justice Gehl was a dedicated public servant and an outstanding jurist whose work on the circuit and supreme benches won the respect and admiration of all who knew him."

Gehl was married to Jessica Colburn and had a daughter, Mary Louise. He died August 28, 1956.

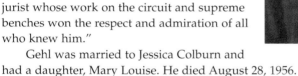

George R. Currie
(1900–1983)
Wisconsin Supreme Court Justice
(1951–1968)
Chief Justice
(1964–1968)

"With a Currie dissent, one knows what is meant and the precedent break that's occurring,
Not so the intent of the cryptic shaft sent with the purring of Currie concurring."
—Attorney Sam Bryan

George R. Currie was born January 16, 1900, in Princeton, Wisconsin. He attended public school in Montello and graduated from Oshkosh State Teachers College in 1919. During his senior year at the University of Wisconsin Law School, he was editor-in-chief of the *Wisconsin Law Review*. He graduated at the top of his class in 1925 and was inducted into the Order of the Coif.

For twenty-six years, Currie practiced law, specializing in corporate law, in Sheboygan. He was appointed to the Wisconsin Supreme Court in 1951 and became chief justice in 1964.

Currie was instrumental in creating the Wisconsin Judicial Conference, which annually brings together members of the state judiciary to "improve the order of justice in this state." He was part of the effort to introduce a Code of Judicial Ethics in 1967, which established governing rules for members of the state judiciary, both on and off the bench.

In 1967, Currie became the first chief justice to be unseated in an election. Although a colleague described him as "the prime intellect on the Supreme Court," several outside factors may have led to his defeat. The mandatory retirement age then in effect for judges would have allowed Currie to serve only only two years of the ten-year term, at which time the governor would have appointed his successor. In addition, a year earlier the Supreme Court made an unpopular ruling that the state could not use its antitrust law to keep the Braves baseball team in Milwaukee. Although Currie had not written the opinion, he had joined it.

After leaving the bench in 1968, Currie lectured at the University of Wisconsin Law School and was voted by the students as Outstanding Teacher of Law. He also served as a reserve judge in Dane County.

In 1971, President Richard Nixon appointed Currie to head the investigative commission for the Office of Economic Opportunity. At the time, the Farm Workers Union was seeking funding from the California Rural Legal Assistance Program. Ronald Reagan, then governor of California, vetoed this funding, and Currie's commission recommended presidential override of the governor's veto, prompting Reagan to characterize Currie as a "radical from a radical state."

A hard-working jurist, Currie relaxed by way of floriculture. He loved to grow dahlias. As a member of the Badger State Dahlia Society and president of the Dahlia Society of Wisconsin, he extended his expertise to dahlia judging. His flowers frequently brightened the tables in the Supreme Court.

Currie and his wife, Gladys Bremer, had two daughters, Janet and Ann. Currie died June 9, 1983, in Madison. At Currie's memorial service, Chief Justice Nathan S. Heffernan said: "It is not an exaggeration to say that it was George Currie who brought the Wisconsin court system out of the dark ages."

Roland J. Steinle
(1896–1966)
Wisconsin Supreme Court Justice
(1954–1958)

"[H]is every action gave evidence of his strength of purpose and inherent sense of right and justice."
—Gregory Gramling, Jr., Steinle's memorial service (1973)

Roland Joseph Steinle was born March 21, 1896, in Milwaukee, shortly after the death of his father, Joseph. Steinle attended high school at Marquette Academy.

Steinle entered Marquette University Law School in 1914 but postponed his studies in 1917 when he became one of the first Marquette students to volunteer in the U.S. Army. While he was in the service, his closest friends were Theodore G. Lewis, John E. Martin, and Edward J. Gehl, all of whom later became justices on the Wisconsin Supreme Court.

After the war, Steinle returned to Marquette, where he earned a law degree in 1920. He practiced law in Milwaukee until 1940, at times serving as a special assistant district attorney of Milwaukee and Forest Counties. On January 2, 1940, Steinle was appointed judge for the Milwaukee County Circuit Court. He was elected in April of that year and was reelected in 1945 and 1951.

Steinle was appointed to the Wisconsin Supreme Court in December 1953 and then was elected to a ten-year term in April 1954. In what was considered a surprise move, Steinle resigned from the bench in March 1958 to become the Republican candidate for the office of U.S. senator, running against William Proxmire. Steinle lost the election. He returned to private practice and served as a circuit court commissioner in Milwaukee, where he remained until his death.

Steinle was one of the few jurists known to be involved in murder trials as a prosecutor, defense attorney, circuit judge, and appellate judge. He loved to teach young lawyers about the law. He worked hard and excelled as a trial lawyer and as a jurist. In his free time, he enjoyed gardening and fishing.

Steinle was married to Helen Sharpe. They had three children: Roland, with whom Steinle practiced law in the years before his death; Betty; and Rosemary. Helen died in December 1953, just one week after Steinle's appointment to the Supreme Court. In 1963, Steinle married Helen's sister Nancy. Steinle died December 22, 1966.

Emmert L. Wingert

(1899–1971)

Wisconsin Supreme Court Justice

(1956–1959)

"Emmert L. Wingert, with all his many talents, was always gentle, soft-spoken and unassuming, but still a giant in the law. He was truly a lawyer's lawyer."
—Chief Justice George R. Currie, Wingert's memorial service (1971)

Emmert "Bill" Laurson Wingert was born April 2, 1899, in Mt. Carroll, Illinois. After serving in World War I, he graduated *Phi Beta Kappa* from Beloit College in 1919. While attending Harvard Law School, he was an editor of the *Harvard Law Review*. He graduated in 1923, returned to Wisconsin, and was admitted to the bar.

Wingert was a staff attorney in the Wisconsin Attorney General's Office until joining a Madison law firm in 1924. While in private practice, he acted as executive counsel to Governor Walter J. Kohler, Sr., from 1929 to 1930.

In 1956, Governor Walter J. Kohler, Jr., appointed Wingert to the Wisconsin Supreme Court. Wingert was an authority in constitutional law. During his twenty-eight months on the Supreme Court, he wrote nearly one hundred opinions. He was defeated in his bid for election in 1958. He was not adept in campaigning, and his loss was attributed in part to his political inexperience. His opponent, William H. Dieterich, had run for statewide office several times and his name was well known. Wingert returned to private law practice and argued several cases before the Wisconsin Supreme Court in the 1960s.

He continued to serve the state in various capacities: he was active in the 1962 reapportionment of state political districts, lectured at the University of Wisconsin Law School, and worked with the Wisconsin Employment Relations Commission.

Justice Horace W. Wilkie commented: "Perhaps the main contribution of Justice Wingert as a member of a collegial court such as the Wisconsin Supreme Court was not only his ability to write sound opinions, but also his role in molding a consensus on the court and in assisting other individual members of the court, both on their basic decisions and their individual opinions."

Wingert's wife, Helen Bridge, was also a lawyer. They had two children, James and Amy. Wingert died February 1, 1971.

E. Harold Hallows
(1904–1974)
Wisconsin Supreme Court Justice
(1958–1974)
Chief Justice
(1968–1974)

*"The legal profession, with its unlimited capacity for good, its high standards
of ethical conduct, its grave responsibilities, its duties and its temptations,
has no place for moral weaklings."*
—Justice E. Harold Hallows, speaking at the University of Wisconsin Law School

E. Harold Hallows was born April 20, 1904, in Fond du Lac, Wisconsin. He received a bachelor's degree in philosophy from Marquette University in 1926. While Hallows was an undergraduate, a professor allowed him to lecture in an upper-level metaphysics class. He entered Columbia University Law School in 1926 but left when he became ill with pneumonia. He returned to law school at the University of Chicago in 1927, where he graduated *cum laude* in 1930.

Hallows was employed as an attorney in Milwaukee and taught at Marquette University Law School for twenty-eight years. He educated hundreds of future lawyers, including Leo B. Hanley and Robert W. Hansen, who later served on the Wisconsin Supreme Court with Hallows. He was president of the Milwaukee Bar Association in 1948 and 1949 and president of the Wisconsin State Bar in 1953.

In 1958, Hallows was appointed to the Wisconsin Supreme Court by Governor Vernon W. Thompson. He retained his seat on the Supreme Court in the 1959 and 1969 elections and became chief justice in 1968. Hallows participated in more than five thousand decisions and wrote nearly seven hundred opinions. "Harold has created a stack of distinguished opinions. Reasoning is serious business to him, and he often shows the results of his experience as a teacher of law," said Justice Thomas E. Fairchild of Hallows in 1970.

Among his many noted opinions, he declared a law requiring children to attend school beyond eighth grade unconstitutional because it violated Amish individuals' first amendment right guaranteeing freedom of religion. The U.S. Supreme Court upheld the decision. Hallows dissented to a state Supreme Court ruling that the father of a child born out of wedlock had no parental rights. His dissent became the basis for the U.S. Supreme Court's decision.

Hallows was diagnosed with acute leukemia in April 1973. He left the Supreme Court in 1974 because of the mandatory retirement age then in effect. Hallows was married to Mary Vivian Hurley and had two children, Mary and Joseph. He died September 11, 1974.

William H. Dieterich
(1897–1964)
Wisconsin Supreme Court Justice
(1959–1964)

"Justice Dieterich could truly be called the People's Lawyer. He was the most compassionate of men and although he represented large corporations he was never happier than when he represented the most indigent of clients for a good cause. . . . Throughout his judicial career, Justice Dieterich never lost sight of his original promise to himself that he would be the People's Lawyer."
—Robert W. Schroeder, Dieterich's memorial service (1965)

William Herbert Dieterich was born December 18, 1897, on his family's farm in Milwaukee County and was educated in the Milwaukee public schools. When the United States declared war on Germany in 1917, he immediately enlisted in the Wisconsin National Guard. He was one of the founders of the American Legion.

When Dieterich returned from war, he attended the University of Wisconsin and the University of Montana and later earned a law degree from Marquette University Law School. He was admitted to the Wisconsin Bar in 1923.

Dieterich was a trial attorney for thirty-six years in Milwaukee and Washington Counties. He served the state and his community as special assistant to the attorney general of Wisconsin, justice of the peace in Washington County, a member of the Board of Governors of the State Bar Foundation, and director of the local school board.

In April 1958, Dieterich defeated Justice Emmert "Bill" Wingert in an election for justice of the Wisconsin Supreme Court. Dieterich had been on the ballot in Wisconsin several times before his victory to the bench. He was unsuccessful in his earlier bids for attorney general and for the Wisconsin Supreme Court.

While on the Supreme Court, Dieterich dissented on a high-profile case, *State v. Sanapaw* (1963). He wrote that notwithstanding the federal Termination Act of 1961, the Menominee Indians kept their rights to hunt and fish on tribal lands free from state game laws. In a different case, *Menominee Tribe v. United States* (1968), the U.S. Supreme Court disagreed with *State v. Sanapaw* and reached the same conclusion as Dieterich's dissent.

Before July 1961, there was no provision for law clerks at the Supreme Court. Dieterich felt there was a need and almost single-handedly persuaded the Wisconsin legislature to authorize the employment of law clerks.

Shortly after his elections to the Supreme Court, Dieterich had "Supreme Court Justice" engraved on his headstone, to ensure that his career on the bench would be known to his descendants, but to the dismay of his superstitious relatives. Dieterich died July 23, 1964. He and his wife, Kathryn Block, had one son, William H. Dieterich III.

Horace W. Wilkie
(1917–1976)
Wisconsin Supreme Court Justice
(1962–1976)
Chief Justice
(1974–1976)

"The degree of civilization we achieve is demonstrated by our system of judicial administration."
—Chief Justice Horace W. Wilkie, Law Day speech (1971)

Horace W. Wilkie was born in Madison on January 9, 1917. He graduated *Phi Beta Kappa* from the University of Wisconsin in 1938 with an economics degree. He earned a law degree from George Washington University in 1944. During the interim, Wilkie studied at the University of Minnesota, American University, and the National Institute of Public Affairs.

After serving in the U.S. Coast Guard during World War II, Wilkie returned to Madison to join his father's law practice. Wilkie chaired the Madison Housing Authority, where he worked to provide adequate public housing in the postwar years. For his efforts, Wilkie received the Madison Junior Chamber of Commerce Outstanding Young Man of the Year award in 1947.

Wilkie was involved with a group who worked to revitalize the state Democratic Party in the late 1940s and 1950s. After three unsuccessful bids for the U.S. Congress, he was elected to the state senate in 1956. He wrote 129 bills, 47 of which became law. Most notable was Wisconsin's first open meetings law. He also spearheaded the first comprehensive court reorganization program since 1848. Wilkie served in the senate until Governor Gaylord A. Nelson appointed him to the Wisconsin Supreme Court in 1962. Wilkie won election to the Supreme Court in 1964 and was reelected in 1974. Later that year, he became the chief justice following the retirement of Chief Justice E. Harold Hallows.

On the bench, he was very proud of writing the 1964 state legislative reapportionment decision, in which the Wisconsin Supreme Court became one of the first state courts in the nation to order reapportionment of legislative districts on the basis of one person, one vote. He campaigned vigorously for court reform to create a one-level trial court system, an intermediate Court of Appeals, and a Supreme Court with authority to suspend or remove judges for just cause. Wilkie believed these changes were key to ensuring justice; they are still in place today.

Wilkie died May 23, 1976, before he was able to see many of his goals for court reform become constitutionally mandated in 1978. Wilkie was married to Marian Beardsley. They had five daughters: Joan, Betsy, Lucy, Christine, and Gretchen. In a footnote to his first financial statement, Wilkie listed his wife and daughters as his most important assets.

Bruce F. Beilfuss

(1915–1986)

Wisconsin Supreme Court Justice

(1964–1983)

Chief Justice

(1976–1983)

*"The two to one victory margin of Justice Bruce Beilfuss of the state Supreme Court
in his re-election last week was a fitting reward for a man who is as well qualified
by temperament, training and rich experience as any man who has served
as a member of the state appeal tribunal in modern times."*
—John Wyngaard, *Green Bay Press-Gazette* (1973)

Bruce Frederich Beilfuss was born January 8, 1915, in Withee, Wisconsin. He graduated from Neilsville High School in 1932 and attended the University of Wisconsin, where he earned an economics degree in 1936 and a law degree in 1938. Beilfuss returned to Clark County in 1938 to practice law and was elected to the Board of Supervisors, the first of fourteen consecutive successful campaigns for public office. He was elected district attorney in 1941.

When World War II broke out, Beilfuss entered the U.S. Navy. While serving as a PT boat commander in the South Pacific, he was reelected Clark County district attorney *in absentia.*

Beilfuss was appointed a circuit judge in 1948 at age thirty-three, becoming the youngest circuit judge in Wisconsin at the time. He served in this capacity for fifteen years. He presided over jury trials in fifty-five of the state's seventy-two counties, traveling as much as thirty thousand miles a year.

While running for the Wisconsin Supreme Court in 1963, Beilfuss defeated four opponents in the primary election and was elected by a two-to-one margin. The Milwaukee Bar Association endorsed Beilfuss with a 99.3-percent approval rating, the highest such score ever recorded.

Beilfuss was reelected by a wide margin in 1973. Upon the death of Chief Justice Horace W. Wilkie in 1976, Beilfuss became the chief justice. An attorney once said of him: "Beilfuss is the man I most respect. He is smarter than the rest. He may not write well, but he has the most clarity. He is a fair man." Beilfuss retired from the Supreme Court in 1983.

Beilfuss was active outside the judiciary. He served as chair on the Board of Visitors of the University of Wisconsin Law School, was a member of the VFW and the American Legion, and was a founder of the Dane County Big Brothers program.

Beilfuss and his first wife, Helene Hendrickson, had one son, Mark. After Helene died, Beilfuss married De Ette Knowlton. He and De Ette raised golden retrievers and greatly loved the outdoors. They adopted a daughter, Karen Johnson. Beilfuss died August 18, 1986.

Leo B. Hanley
(1908–1994)
Wisconsin Supreme Court Justice
(1966–1978)

"In such a noisy place as the law, Hanley long has been known as the quiet man."
—William Jane, *Milwaukee Sentinel* (1976)

Leo B. Hanley was born April 27, 1908, in Milwaukee. He attended Milwaukee public schools and graduated from Marquette University Law School in 1933, during the depths of the Great Depression. He paid his way through school by working at the Wisconsin Club.

Hanley was appointed assistant city attorney for Milwaukee in 1936. He was commanding officer of the USS *Wildwood* during World War II, transporting bombs to Europe. After the war, he returned to the city attorney's office.

In February 1949, Hanley was appointed a civil court judge for Milwaukee County. He was later elected to the circuit court and became the chief judge. He served as chair of the Milwaukee Board of Judges from 1955 to 1956.

Hanley was a widely respected trial judge and was often referred to as "the great conciliator" because of his ability to settle cases before trial. He was soft-spoken and even-tempered. Someone once said that if Hanley jumped into a swimming pool, he would not make a wave.

Governor Warren P. Knowles appointed Hanley to the Wisconsin Supreme Court in 1966. Hanley was elected in 1968. At Hanley's memorial service, Justice John L. Coffey, who appeared before Hanley as a lawyer in trial court and later served on the state Supreme Court, said: "Leo was successful in life because he was imbued with a wonderful dedication to his family, his church and his country, as exemplified by his 57 years in government service; 44 years on the judiciary. . . . As a judge, he was always prepared, often knowing the subject matter better than we litigators."

Justice Donald W. Steinmetz said of Hanley at the memorial: "He worked very hard: he wrote 492 majority opinions; he participated in 40 concurrences and dissents. He is remembered for his demeanor, patience. I never saw him in any but a pleasant manner."

Hanley retired at the end of his term in 1978. He and his wife, Sophia Wabiszewski, had three sons, James, Robert, and Dennis, all of whom graduated from Marquette University Law School. Hanley died May 12, 1994.

Connor T. Hansen
(1913–1987)
Wisconsin Supreme Court Justice
(1967–1980)

"I remember his ever-present bow tie, his love of growing roses and herbs, and his affection for the common man. As a Sibelius symphony, Connor's strength grew out of the earth, in his case the populist soil of Wisconsin. He was a good judge."
—Judge Thomas H. Barland, Hansen's memorial service (1988)

Connor Theodore Hansen was born November 1, 1913, in Freeman, South Dakota. In 1934, he graduated from the Eau Claire State Teachers College, now the University of Wisconsin–Eau Claire. He earned a law degree from the University of Wisconsin Law School in 1937.

Hansen was elected district attorney of Eau Claire County in 1938 and served until 1943. During World War II, he was a special agent in the FBI. After the war, Hansen returned to private practice in Eau Claire and was elected to the Eau Claire County Board, where he served from 1947 to 1957. He ran unsuccessfully as the Republican candidate for U.S. Congress in 1948.

Judge Thomas H. Barland said at Hansen's memorial service: "Congress beckoned in 1948, but that proved to be one of his few unsuccessful political efforts. He

would not have been happy in Congress . . . his Wisconsin and Eau Claire roots were too deep."

Governor Vernon W. Thompson appointed Hansen to the Eau Claire County Court in 1958. He was reputed for his work in juvenile court and his efforts to help high school dropouts.

In 1967, Governor Warren P. Knowles appointed Hansen to the Wisconsin Supreme Court, making him the first justice appointed directly from county court and the first justice from Eau Claire County. Hansen was elected to a full term on the Supreme Court in 1970.

Controversy arose in 1973 when Hansen was elected to the Lake Mills City Council. Critics argued that the Wisconsin Constitution makes it illegal for judges to hold other political offices. A week after the city council election, Hansen declined the position.

At the end of his term, Hansen did not seek reelection. Because of the mandatory retirement age then in effect, he could not finish another full term and he did not want the governor to appoint his replacement. He retired in 1980.

Hansen was married to Annette Phillips Ferry. They had four children: Annette, Peter, David, and Jane. He died August 21, 1987.

Robert W. Hansen

(1911–1997)

Wisconsin Supreme Court Justice

(1968–1978)

"Hansen is the colorful justice—in appearance, personality, judicial attitude, individuality."
—*Milwaukee Journal* (1976)

Robert Wayne Hansen was born April 29, 1911, in Milwaukee. He graduated *magna cum laude* from Marquette University Law School in 1933.

Hansen was devoted to the Eagles organization. At twenty-seven, he was elected chapter president and became the youngest state president and national president of the Eagles. He served as editor of the *Eagle,* the order's national magazine. He resigned as editor over a differing opinion with other members in 1950. He said the organization was becoming "an insurance company more than a fraternal organization." He resumed the editorship in 1953.

In 1951, Hansen became chief examiner of the Milwaukee Board of Fire and Police Commissioners, where he worked until his appointment to Milwaukee County District Court in 1954. He served as circuit judge in the family court division from 1961 to 1968.

In April 1967, Hansen defeated state Supreme Court Chief Justice George R. Currie, becoming the first candidate to unseat a chief justice. While campaigning, Hansen noted that Currie, then sixty-seven, could serve only a little more than two years of a ten-year term because of the mandatory retirement age then in effect for judges.

On the Supreme Court, Hansen was known for his colloquial writing style. In one decision involving obscenity and redeeming social value, Hansen wrote: "An orange floating in an open sewer does not change it to fruit salad."

In 1977, Hansen chose not to seek reelection. When asked why, he said: "A little bit of the bubble has gone out of the champagne." He also noted that the mandatory retirement age then in effect would allow him to serve only about three years of the ten-year term. Upon Hansen's retirement, the *Milwaukee Journal* referred to him as "an unorthodox gent who has been known to walk, lost deep in thought, in stocking feet in the Supreme Court chambers."

Hansen and his wife, Dorothy, had four children: Susan, John, James, and Karen. He died on June 9, 1997.

Thomas E. Fairchild

(1912–)

Wisconsin Supreme Court Justice

(1956–1966)

Thomas E. Fairchild was born on Christmas 1912 in Milwaukee. After studying at Deep Springs College in California, Princeton University, and Cornell University, he received his A.B. from Cornell University in 1934 and his L.L.B. from the University of Wisconsin Law School in 1938.

Fairchild practiced law in Portage from 1938 to 1942 with Daniel H. Grady, a longtime member of the University of Wisconsin Board of Regents. He served from 1942 to 1945 as an attorney with the U.S. Office of Price Administration, dealing with consumer rationing. For the next three years, he practiced law in Milwaukee.

In 1948, Fairchild joined others working to revitalize the state Democratic Party, which had seldom won offices since the 1890s, and he ran in elections in 1948, 1950, and 1952. He was elected attorney general in 1948. His 1950 bid for the office of U.S. senator against incumbent Alexander Wiley was hampered by his unpopular decision as attorney general to outlaw "Stop the Music," a radio show awarding big prizes.

President Harry S. Truman appointed Fairchild U.S. attorney for the Western District of Wisconsin in 1951. Fairchild resigned in 1952 and ran unsuccessfully for the U.S. Senate against Senator Joseph McCarthy. Fairchild returned to private law practice in Milwaukee. In 1956, he and others of the Milwaukee Bar Association appeared as counsel for alleged communists subpoenaed before the House Un-American Activities Committee.

Fairchild was elected to the Wisconsin Supreme Court in April 1956 and served until 1966, when he was appointed by President Lyndon B. Johnson to join the U.S. Court of Appeals for the 7th Circuit. He was chief judge from 1975 to 1981 and has been a senior judge since then. From 1997 to 2000, he was chair of the Commission on Judicial Campaigns and Ethics, appointed by the Wisconsin Supreme Court. Fairchild is also a member of the council of the American Law Institute.

Thomas and Eleanor Fairchild have four children and eight grandchildren.

Myron L. Gordon

(1918–)

Wisconsin Supreme Court Justice

(1962–1967)

M yron L. Gordon was born February 11, 1918, in Kenosha, Wisconsin. He graduated *Phi Beta Kappa* with bachelor's and master's degrees from the University of Wisconsin in 1939. He earned his law degree from Harvard Law School in 1942 and was in private law practice in Milwaukee for the next eight years.

Gordon was a lieutenant in the U.S. Naval Reserves from 1944 to 1946. He later became a member of the Disabled American Veterans and was state commander in 1959. He was president of the Milwaukee Hearing Society from 1951 to 1953. From 1950 to 1954, Gordon was a Milwaukee County Civil Court judge and a Milwaukee County Circuit Court judge from 1954 to 1961. He was elected to the Wisconsin Supreme Court in 1961.

Known as a "picturesque writer," Gordon occasionally included poetry or Shakespearean references in his opinions. He served on the Supreme Court until 1967, when President Lyndon B. Johnson appointed him as a federal district court judge for the Eastern District of Wisconsin. Gordon serves as the senior judge.

In 1992, *Milwaukee Magazine* gave Gordon high ratings for scholarship and decisiveness. "He borders on genius," said one lawyer. "He's able to cut through very complex issues and get to the meat of the issue. He understands the law completely."

In 1998, the *Almanac of the Federal Judiciary* printed the following: "During trial, lawyers said Gordon runs a tight ship: 'He's the epitome of a judge who rules with an iron fist, but it is a fair fist.'" After fifty years as a judge, Gordon retired in January 2000. Both the Milwaukee Bar Association and the State Bar of Wisconsin presented him their Lifetime Achievement Awards after his retirement.

Gordon's first wife, Peggy, died in 1973. They had three children: Wendy, John, and Polly. Gordon was remarried, to Myra, in 1979.

Nathan S. Heffernan

(1920–)

Wisconsin Supreme Court Justice

(1964–1995)

Chief Justice

(1983–1995)

Nathan Stewart Heffernan was born August 6, 1920, in Frederic, Wisconsin. He attended school in Sheboygan and graduated from the University of Wisconsin in 1942. During World War II, Heffernan took time out of his studies to serve in the U.S. Navy. He later attended the Harvard Graduate School of Business and graduated Order of the Coif from the University of Wisconsin Law School in 1948.

From 1948 to 1959, Heffernan was in private law practice in Sheboygan at the firm of Buchen & Heffernan. He served as assistant district attorney in Sheboygan County from 1951 to 1953 and city attorney of Sheboygan from 1953 to 1959. Heffernan became Wisconsin's deputy attorney general in 1959 and served in that capacity until 1962 when President John F. Kennedy appointed him as U.S. Attorney for the Western District of Wisconsin. In 1964, Governor John W. Reynolds appointed Heffernan, age forty-three, to the Wisconsin Supreme Court. Heffernan became the chief justice in 1983.

Heffernan's work on the bench distinguished him as a top scholar with eclectic opinions and a "puckish" sense of humor. He is well known for his commitment to civil liberties and women's rights and is recognized for his involvement in the court reorganization of 1978, which created a Wisconsin Court of Appeals. Heffernan taught summer courses on appellate administration and opinion writing at New York University Law School and was an adjunct professor of appellate practice and procedure at the University of Wisconsin Law School for fifteen years.

Heffernan retired in 1995. His thirty-one years on the Supreme Court make him the third-longest-serving judge in Wisconsin history. He told the *Milwaukee Journal,* "For me, it has been the fulfillment of my aspirations as a lawyer and a continuing opportunity to render worthwhile public service. . . . But it's time to step down and enjoy life."

Heffernan and his wife, Dorothy Hillemann, have three children: Katie, Michael, and Thomas.

Roland B. Day

(1919–)

Wisconsin Supreme Court Justice

(1974–1996)

Chief Justice

(1995–1996)

Roland B. Day was born June 11, 1919, in Oshkosh, Wisconsin, and was raised in Eau Claire. He received a bachelor's degree in 1942 and a law degree in 1947, both from the University of Wisconsin. He served overseas in the U.S. Army during World War II.

Day was a law trainee in the Office of the Attorney General in 1947 and was the first assistant district attorney for Dane County from 1949 to 1952. From 1957 to 1958, he served as legal counsel to Senator William Proxmire in Washington, D.C.

Upon returning to Madison, Day resumed law practice until 1974. During this period, he was chair of the Madison Public Housing Authority, which during his tenure built the first public housing units in Madison; and he served as special counsel to Governor John W. Reynolds in the reapportionment case before the Wisconsin Supreme Court, which became the first state court in the nation to reapportion legislative districts on the basis of one person, one vote. He also represented the mayor of Madison in a civil action challenging his right to go forward with the building of the Monona Terrace Civic Center and served on the Board of Regents of the University of Wisconsin System from 1972 to 1974.

In 1974, while a partner in the law firm of Wheeler, Van Sickle, Day and Anderson, Day was appointed to the Wisconsin Supreme Court by Governor Patrick J. Lucey. He was elected in 1976 and was reelected in 1986. He became the chief justice on August 1, 1995, and retired a year later, at the end of his second term.

While on the Supreme Court, Day was a member of the Judicial Council and the Council of Criminal Justice. From 1986 to 1991, Day served as state chair of the Wisconsin Bicentennial Committee on the U.S. Constitution. His name appears on a bicentennial commemorative plaque in the capitol rotunda, along with an original copy of the Wisconsin Constitution of 1848.

In 2002, at the request of Bishop William Bullock, Day became chair of the Madison Catholic Diocese Review Board on Sexual Abuse.

Day is married to Mary Jane Purcell. They have one daughter, Sarah.

William G. Callow

(1921–)

Wisconsin Supreme Court Justice

(1977–1992)

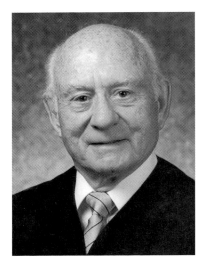

William Grant Callow was born April 9, 1921, in Waukesha, Wisconsin. He graduated from Waukesha High School in 1939. He earned a bachelor's degree in economics in 1943 and a law degree in 1948, both from the University of Wisconsin. Callow served in the U.S. Marine Corps during World War II and in the U.S. Air Force during the Korean Conflict.

From 1952 to 1960, Callow served as city attorney in Waukesha. He was elected judge for Waukesha County court three times between 1961 and 1973. In 1967, he was appointed a Wisconsin Commissioner for the National Conference of Commissioners on Uniform State Laws, and he serves in that capacity to date.

As a trial judge, Callow pioneered group therapy for drunk drivers and victim/offender reconciliation in property crime cases. He lectured to more than three hundred Wisconsin high schools on the subject of teenage marriage, misconduct, and the law. He also wrote two related booklets for the State Bar of Wisconsin.

Callow won a seat on the Wisconsin Supreme Court in 1977. He is the only county judge to have been elected directly to the state Supreme Court. He was reelected in 1987. Callow served on the faculty for the Wisconsin Judicial College and the National Judicial College. He also lectured at the University of Wisconsin and Marquette University Law Schools. Among his many honors, Callow is an elected fellow of the American Bar Foundation and was the first graduate of Waukesha High School to be elected to the school's Wall of Fame. In addition, the University of Wisconsin recognized him with its Outstanding Wisconsin Alumnus award.

Callow retired from the Supreme Court in 1992 and remains active in the judiciary. He serves as a reserve judge, is an arbitrator/mediator for the Wisconsin Employment Relations Commission, and mediates disputes nationwide and abroad.

Callow enjoys golf, boating, and antique cars. He is married and has three children.

John L. Coffey
(1922–)
Wisconsin Supreme Court Justice
(1978–1981)

John L. Coffey was born April 15, 1922, in Milwaukee. He graduated from Marquette University in 1943. During World War II, he served in the U.S. Navy. He then returned to Marquette University Law School and graduated in 1948.

Coffey was appointed assistant city attorney in 1949 and served until 1954 when he was elected a civil court judge for Milwaukee County. He was elected a municipal judge in 1960 and served until the court reorganization in 1962, when he was elected a circuit judge for Milwaukee County. During his sixteen years on the bench in Milwaukee, he served as senior judge and chief presiding judge in the felony division as well as a judge in the civil division.

In 1977, Coffey campaigned for the open seat on the Wisconsin Supreme Court. As part of his campaign, Coffey said that judges needed flexibility in sentencing, while his opponent favored determinate sentencing. After winning the election, Coffey told the *Milwaukee Journal* that the vote was a clear message to the state legislature that "the people of Wisconsin are interested in a system where there is an equal balance between the rights of the defendant and society."

Among his many honors, Coffey was selected as the Outstanding Man of the Year by the Milwaukee Junior Chamber of Commerce in 1951. In 1980, he was chosen Marquette University Outstanding Law Alumnus of the Year and was selected for membership in *Alpha Sigma Nu* (National Honor Society). In 1985, he received the Marquette University Alumni Association Merit Award for distinguished professional achievement.

Coffey was appointed for life to the U.S. Court of Appeals for the 7th Circuit in 1981 by President Ronald Reagan. The 1994 edition of *The American Bench* lists more than fifty important decisions that he wrote as a U.S. Court of Appeals judge.

Coffey is married to Marion Kunzelmann and has two children, Peter Coffey and Elizabeth Mary Coffey Robbins.

Louis J. Ceci
(1927–)
Wisconsin Supreme Court Justice
(1982–1993)

L ouis J. Ceci was born September 10, 1927, in New York City. In 1941, he moved to Milwaukee. In 1945, at age seventeen, he enlisted in the U.S. Navy and served in the Southwest Pacific during World War II.

Ceci graduated from Theodore Roosevelt Evening High School (NYC) in 1947 and earned a bachelor's degree in philosophy and a law degree from Marquette University in 1951 and 1954, respectively. He immediately began his own law practice and then served as a principal assistant city attorney of Milwaukee from 1958 to 1963.

In 1964, Ceci successfully ran for the state assembly. He was the Republican candidate for attorney general in 1966. He was appointed county judge for Milwaukee County in 1968 and was elected to that seat a year later. In 1973, he was elected to the Milwaukee County Circuit Court. He served as presiding judge of the civil division of Milwaukee from 1980 to 1982.

While on the bench, Ceci was an active lecturer for the state judicial conferences. He served as delegate to the Trial Judges Association of the American Bar Association and was coauthor of the standards of judicial education adopted by the American Bar Association in 1982.

When Ceci ran for the Wisconsin Supreme Court in 1980, he was defeated by fewer than five thousand votes out of 1.3 million cast. Governor Lee S. Dreyfus appointed Ceci to the Supreme Court in 1982 and said he was "pleased to be able to appoint someone who has already received 658,000 votes from the people of this state."

Ceci was unopposed when he ran for a ten-year Supreme Court term in 1984. In September 1993, after thirty-two years of public service, Ceci stepped down from the Supreme Court to spend more time with his family. He currently serves as a reserve judge for Wisconsin and is a certified mediator.

When he is not golfing, Ceci and his wife, Shirley, enjoy traveling. Ceci has been married twice and has six children and eight grandchildren.

Janine P. Geske
(1949–)
Wisconsin Supreme Court Justice
(1993–1998)

Janine P. Geske was born May 12, 1949, in Port Washington, Wisconsin, and raised in Cedarburg. She received bachelor's and master's degrees from Beloit College in 1971 and a law degree from Marquette University School of Law in 1975. Geske then became the chief staff attorney for the Legal Aid Society of Milwaukee, where she worked until 1979. She was an assistant professor at Marquette University Law School from 1978 to 1981 and was the director of the Marquette University Law School's Clinic for the Elderly, which she founded.

Beginning in 1981, Geske served in the Milwaukee County Circuit Court for twelve years, until she was appointed to the Wisconsin Supreme Court by Governor Tommy G. Thompson in 1993. She won election to the court in 1994.

In February 1998, Geske announced her resignation from the Supreme Court effective in September 1998. She left the bench to start her own alternative dispute resolution practice, to teach, and to become more involved in the community. She joined the faculty of Marquette Law School as a distinguished professor of law and was named interim dean of the law school following the sudden death of Dean Howard Eisenberg. From February to May 2002, Geske also served as Milwaukee County executive, stepping in to fill the void until voters could elect a replacement for longtime County Executive F. Thomas Ament.

Geske was on the faculty of the National Judicial College and served as dean of the Wisconsin Judicial College. She is a fellow in the American Bar Association, a member of the American Law Institute, and a member of the Society for Professionals in Dispute Resolution and the National Association of Women Judges. She received both the Marquette Law School Alumnae Award and the Alumna of the Year award for Marquette University.

Geske is married to Michael J. Hogan and has three children: Mia, Sarah, and Kevin.

Donald W. Steinmetz

(1924–)

Wisconsin Supreme Court Justice

(1980–1999)

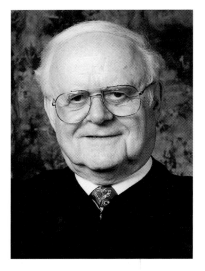

D onald W. Steinmetz was born September 19, 1924, in Milwaukee. He received a bachelor's degree from the University of Wisconsin in 1949 and a law degree from the University of Wisconsin Law School in 1951.

Steinmetz was in private law practice in Milwaukee for seven years before becoming an assistant city attorney in Milwaukee in 1958. In 1960, he became first assistant district attorney for Milwaukee County; he served in that role until 1966, when he became a county judge for Milwaukee County. He served in county court and later in circuit court until 1980, when he was elected to the Wisconsin Supreme Court. He was reelected in 1990 and retired in 1999 with one year left in his term.

Steinmetz served on the Judicial Council, the Judicial Education and Selection Committee, and the committee that recommended rules on the use of sound camera equipment in the courtroom.

Steinmetz and his wife, Marjorie, have five children: Mary, Kathleen, Chris, Susan, and James, and thirteen grandchildren.

Shirley S. Abrahamson

(1933–)

Wisconsin Supreme Court Justice

(1976–present)

Chief Justice

(1996–present)

S hirley S. Abrahamson was born December 17, 1933, in New York City. She received bachelor's degrees from New York University in 1953, a law degree from the Indiana University Law School in 1956, and a doctor of juridical science in American legal history from the University of Wisconsin Law School in 1962.

Abrahamson was in private law practice in Madison for fourteen years and was a professor of law at the University of Wisconsin Law School. She also has taught at Marquette University Law School. She has served on the Wisconsin Supreme Court since Governor Patrick J. Lucey appointed her in 1976. She was the first woman to serve on the Supreme Court. She was elected to the Supreme Court in 1979 and reelected in 1989 and 1999. She has been the chief justice since August 1, 1996.

Abrahamson was a member of the U.S. Department of Justice (FBI) DNA Advisory Board and chair of the National Commission on the Future of DNA Evidence of the National Institute of Justice. She is a member of the Council of the American Law Institute, the board of directors of the Institute of Judicial Administration (New York University Law School), and the American Bar Association Standing Committee on Professional Discipline. She was elected first vice president of the National Conference of Chief Justices and also is a member of the Board of Directors of the National Center for State Courts. In addition, she served on the State Bar of Wisconsin's Commission on the Delivery of Legal Services.

Abrahamson is the recipient of fourteen honorary doctors of law degrees and the Distinguished Alumni Award of the University of Wisconsin. She is a fellow of the Wisconsin Academy Sciences, Arts & Letters and of the American Academy of Arts and Sciences and is an elected member of the American Philosophical Society.

Abrahamson and her husband, Seymour, have a son, Daniel.

William A. Bablitch

(1941–)

Wisconsin Supreme Court Justice

(1983–present)

William A. Bablitch was born on March 1, 1941, in Stevens Point, Wisconsin. He studied at the University of Wisconsin–Stevens Point and received a bachelor's degree from the University of Wisconsin in 1963. He served in the Peace Corps for two years before earning a law degree from the University of Wisconsin Law School in 1968 and a master of law degree in the appellate process from the University of Virginia School of Law in 1987.

Bablitch was Portage County district attorney from 1969 to 1972 and served in the Wisconsin senate from 1972 to 1983. During his tenure in the senate, he served as president *pro tempore* and majority leader. He was elected to the Wisconsin Supreme Court in 1983 and reelected in 1993. In December 2001, he announced his intention to retire at the end of his current term on July 31, 2003.

While on the court, Bablitch has served on the Board of Visitors of the University of Wisconsin Law School and the University of Wisconsin–Stevens Point. He was on the faculty at the New York University Law School Institute of Judicial Administration and is a frequent guest lecturer to various groups around the country, including the Arizona, Florida, Indiana, and Kentucky Supreme Courts.

Bablitch is married to Ann Milne and has one daughter, Bulleh.

Jon P. Wilcox

(1936–)

Wisconsin Supreme Court Justice

(1992–present)

J on P. Wilcox was born in Berlin, Wisconsin, on September 5, 1936, and was raised in Wild Rose. He received his bachelor's degree from Ripon College in 1958. He served as an officer in the U.S. Army for two years before earning a law degree from the University of Wisconsin Law School in 1965.

Wilcox was in private law practice for fourteen years and started his own law firm. He served three terms in the Wisconsin assembly from 1969 to 1975. In 1979, he was elected circuit court judge in Waushara County, a position he held until 1992. He served as chief judge of the 6th Judicial District for seven years, chair of the Wisconsin Committee of Chief Judges, and chair of the Wisconsin Sentencing Commission from 1987 to 1992. He was appointed to the Wisconsin Supreme Court in 1992 and elected in 1997.

Wilcox is a member of the State Bar of Wisconsin Media–Law Relations Committee and Bench Bar Committee, co-chair of the Jurist Award Subcommittee, and co-chair of the Commission of the Judiciary as a Co-Equal Branch of Government. He also serves on the Wisconsin Judicial Council, the State-Federal Judicial Council, and the Board of Directors of the Wisconsin Law Foundation. He is a member of the American Bar Association Committee on Continuing Appellate Education and has been elected a fellow of the American Bar Foundation. Wilcox has been a faculty member of the Wisconsin Judicial College since 1985. He is a recipient of the Ripon College Distinguished Alumni Award.

Wilcox and his wife, Jane Ann, have two children, Jeffrey and Jennifer.

Ann Walsh Bradley

(1950–)

Wisconsin Supreme Court Justice

(1995–present)

A nn Walsh Bradley was born July 5, 1950, in Richland Center, Wisconsin. She received a bachelor's degree in 1972 from Webster College in St. Louis. She was a high school teacher before entering the University of Wisconsin Law School, where she earned a law degree in 1976.

Bradley was in private law practice until becoming a circuit court judge in Marathon County in 1985. She was elected to the Wisconsin Supreme Court in 1995.

Bradley is a member of the American Law Institute, a former associate dean and faculty member of the Wisconsin Judicial College, a former chair of the Wisconsin Judicial Conference, and a former board member of the National Association of Women Judges. She serves on the University of Wisconsin Board of Visitors.

Bradley and her husband, Mark, have four children: Bryn, John, Elizabeth, and Patrick.

N. Patrick Crooks

(1938–)

Wisconsin Supreme Court Justice

(1996–present)

N. Patrick Crooks was born in Green Bay, Wisconsin, in 1938. He earned a bachelor's degree from St. Norbert College in 1960 and a law degree from the University of Notre Dame in 1963.

Before joining the Wisconsin Supreme Court in 1996, Crooks served nineteen years on the bench in Brown County and worked in private practice in 1963 and again from 1966 to 1977. From 1964 to 1966, he served as a U.S. Army officer at the Pentagon, assigned to the office of the Judge Advocate General. While in private practice, he taught business law at the University of Wisconsin–Green Bay.

Crooks was named Trial Judge of the Year by the Wisconsin Chapter of the American Board of Trial Advocates in 1994. That same year, Governor Tommy G. Thompson appointed him to serve on a special task force to revise Wisconsin's juvenile justice code. Crooks is a director of the Notre Dame Law Association, a member of the executive committee of the Wisconsin Law Foundation Board, and a law school evaluator for the American Bar Association's Legal Education and Admissions Section. He is also a member of the American Bar Association Appellate Judges Section, the State Bar of Wisconsin's Media–Law Relations Committee, the Wisconsin Judicial Council, and the James E. Doyle Chapter of the American Inns of Court.

Crooks and his wife, Kristin, have six children, five of whom are lawyers.

David Prosser, Jr.

(1942–)

Wisconsin Supreme Court Justice

(1998–present)

David Prosser, Jr., was born in Chicago on December 24, 1942, and raised in Appleton, Wisconsin. He received a bachelor's degree from DePauw University in 1965 and a law degree from the University of Wisconsin Law School in 1968.

Prosser was appointed to the Supreme Court in 1998 by Governor Tommy G. Thompson to fill the vacancy created upon Justice Janine P. Geske's resignation. He ran unopposed in the April 2001 election.

Before joining the Supreme Court, Prosser served on the Wisconsin Tax Appeals Commission, where he conducted hearings and issued decisions on a variety of disputes related to Wisconsin taxation. Prosser was appointed to the Tax Appeals Commission following eighteen years in the Wisconsin legislature. Prosser represented the Appleton area in the state assembly from 1979 through 1996. During his tenure, he served six years as assembly minority leader and two years as assembly speaker. For fourteen years, he was a legislative member of the National Conference of Commissioners on Uniform State Laws.

Prior to his election to the assembly, Prosser served as Outagamie County district attorney. He also worked in Washington, D.C., first as an attorney/advisor in the U.S. Department of Justice's Office of Criminal Justice, then as administrative assistant to Congressman Harold Froehlich, who was a member of the House Judiciary Committee during the Watergate impeachment inquiry.

Diane S. Sykes

(1957–)

Wisconsin Supreme Court Justice

(1999–present)

D iane S. Sykes was born December 23, 1957, and raised in the Milwaukee area. Sykes received a bachelor's degree from the Medill School of Journalism at Northwestern University in 1980 and a law degree from Marquette University Law School in 1984. Between college and law school, Justice Sykes worked as a reporter for the *Milwaukee Journal*.

Sykes was appointed to the Supreme Court in September 1999 by Governor Tommy G. Thompson to replace Justice Donald Steinmetz, who retired one year before the end of his second term on the Supreme Court. Sykes was elected to a ten-year term in April 2000.

Before joining the Supreme Court, Sykes was a Milwaukee County Circuit Court judge from 1992 to 1999. While on the trial court bench, Sykes served in the misdemeanor, felony, and civil divisions. Prior to her election to the Milwaukee County Circuit Court, Sykes practiced law with the Milwaukee law firm of Whyte & Hirschboeck S.C. and served as law clerk to Federal Judge Terence T. Evans.

Sykes is the mother of two sons, Jay and Alexander.

Bibliography

"Chief Justice Horace W. Wilkie Dies." *Wisconsin Bar Bulletin*. (Madison: State Bar of Wisconsin, June 1976)

"Go and Study Law." *Wisconsin Then and Now*. (Madison: State Historical Society of Wisconsin, October 1957)

"Rosenberry Memorial Presented for State Bar." *Wisconsin Bar Bulletin*. (Madison: State Bar of Wisconsin, February 1962)

Beilfuss, Bruce F. "Justice Horace W. Wilkie." *Wisconsin Law Review*, 1976, No. 3

Berryman, John R. *History of the Bench and Bar of Wisconsin*, Vols. 1, 2. (Chicago: H. C. Cooper, Jr., & Co., 1898)

Brown, William Fiske. *Rock County, Wisconsin: A New History of its Cities, Villages, Towns, Citizens and Varied Interests, from the Earliest Times, up-to-date*, pp. 514–516. (Chicago: C. F. Cooper, Jr., & Co., 1908)

Capital Times. March 20, 1946; June 20, 1949; August 20, 1954; February 15, 1958; October 20, 1959; February 1, 1971; February 2, 1971; July 27, 1973; July 30, 1973; February 25, 1976; May 24, 1976; May 27, 1976; August 6, 1979

Current, Richard N. "The Civil War Era, 1848–1873." *The History of Wisconsin*, Vol. 2. (Madison: State Historical Society of Wisconsin, 1976)

Fairchild, Thomas E. *Recollections of the Court* (Madison: Wisconsin Supreme Court History Collection, 1998)

Green Bay Press-Gazette. December 24, 1972; February 4, 1973; April 12, 1973; July 4, 1974; February 29, 1976; May 25, 1976; May 28, 1976

Higgins, Timothy. "Justices of the Wisconsin Supreme Court." *Wisconsin Law Review*, July 1949

In Memoriam. Memorial address for each deceased justice given by the State Bar of Wisconsin and published in *Wisconsin Reports*

La Crosse Tribune. July 9, 1974

Langill, Ellen. "Levi Hubbell and the Wisconsin Judiciary: A Dilemma in Legal Ethics and Non-Partisan Judicial Elections." *Marquette Law Review*, 1998

Lucey, Patrick J. "Testimonial to the Late Chief Justice Horace W. Wilkie." *Wisconsin Law Review*, 1976, No. 3

McGalloway, John P. "Supreme Court Centennial: The History and Achievements of a Great Court in the First Century of its Existence." *Wisconsin Reports*, Vol. 264. June 1953

Milwaukee Journal. February 16, 1958; May 19, 1962; February 1, 1971; June 28, 1974; August 5, 1974; September 12, 1974; September 15, 1974; December 19, 1975; February 25, 1976; March 17, 1976; May 25, 1976; May 27, 1976; December 1, 1977

Milwaukee Sentinel. December 22, 1966; December 13, 1968; July 30, 1973; August 1, 1973; February 25, 1976; May 24, 1976; May 27, 1976

Paine, Byron. *Unconstitutionality of the Fugitive Slave Act.* (Milwaukee: Free Democrat Office, 1854)

Pinney, Silas U. "Biographical Sketches of the Judges of the First Supreme Court." *Wisconsin Reports,* Vol. 3. (Chicago: Callaghan & Company, Law Publishers, 1876)

Racine Journal Times. October 19, 1972; April 2, 1973

Raney, William Francis. *Wisconsin: A Story of Progress.* (New York: Prentice-Hall, Inc., 1940)

Ranney, Joseph A. "Molders and Shapers of Wisconsin Law: Chief Justices Edward G. Ryan and Luther S. Dixon." *Wisconsin Lawyer.* (Madison: State Bar of Wisconsin, March 1993)

Reed, Parker McCobb. *The Bench and Bar of Wisconsin.* (Milwaukee: P. M. Reed, 1882)

Rosenberry, Marvin B. *Personal Papers from 1845–1956.* (Madison: Wisconsin Supreme Court History Collection)

Ryan, Edward G., *Personal Papers from 1815–1902.* (Madison: Wisconsin Supreme Court History Collection, 1998)

Schafer, Joseph. "William Penn Lyon." *Wisconsin Magazine of History,* Vol. 9. 1925–1926

Sheboygan Press. June 25, 1949; December 29, 1967; January 6, 1968; August 8, 1974

State Historical Society of Wisconsin. *Dictionary of Wisconsin Biography.* (Milwaukee: The North American Press, 1960)

Wilkie, Horace W. "A Tribute to Wisconsin's Fiftieth Justice: Remarks of Justice Horace W. Wilkie." *Wisconsin Bar Bulletin.* (Madison: State Bar of Wisconsin, October 1974)

Winslow, John Bradley. *The Story of a Great Court.* (Chicago: T. H. Flood & Co., 1912)

Wisconsin Legislative Reference Bureau. *Blue Book.* 1997–1998 and previous editions dating to 1856

Wisconsin State Journal. January 11, 1898; January 12, 1898; January 11, 1943; March 19, 1946; December 24, 1946; December 30, 1949; August 29, 1956; February 2, 1958; February 15, 1958; February 2, 1971; June 23, 1971; May 16, 1972; March 12, 1973; August 2, 1974; September 3, 1974; December 20, 1975; January 3, 1976; May 24, 1976; May 27, 1976; August 7, 1979